The Awakening o.

A Foremost Necessity

Michele Doucette

The Awakening of Humanity: A Foremost Necessity

ISBN 978-1-935786-20-7

Printed in the United States of America by

St. Clair Publications

PO Box 726

McMinnville, TN   37111-0726

http://stan.stclair.net

Cover image © Aleksandr Matveev (of Moscow)

http://www.flickr.com/photos/27351229@N04/

Awareness means you come with an inner light, you move fully alert. Each step is taken in awareness; everything is done in full awareness. If you are aware, you speak with awareness, but the awareness comes from the inward being. It flows from the inner being towards others. Awareness is an inner quality of consciousness; it has nothing to do with closed or open eyes. Walk, with awareness. Eat, with awareness. Breathe, with awareness. The ego is nothing but condensed unawareness. When you become aware, by and by that condensed unawareness we call 'ego' disappears. Just as if you bring a lamp into the room, and the darkness disappears. Awareness is the lamp; be a lamp unto yourself. Awareness is the greatest alchemy there is. Just go on becoming more and more aware, and you will find your life changing for the better in every possible dimension. It will bring great fulfillment.

Osho

Table of Contents

If you aspire to become an evolutionarily enlightened human being, your ability to do so depends upon accepting the simple fact that independent of external circumstances, *you always have a measure of freedom to choose.*

That sounds like a simple statement, but it's amazing how many intelligent people will deny it. When you look honestly for yourself, however, you will see that it is true: you are *always* choosing.

Sometimes your choices are conscious; sometimes they are unconscious.

Sometimes they are inspired by the best parts of yourself; other times they are motivated by lower impulses and instincts.

But the bottom line is that *every time you act or react, at some level, a choice is being made.*

And you, whoever you are, are the one who is making that choice.

After all, who else could it be?

Andrew Cohen (editor of EnlightenNext Magazine)

Author's Note

In the words of Andrew Cohen, editor of EnlightenNext Magazine ... *I don't believe the purpose of life is to just be happy.*

Why would God take fourteen billion years to produce highly evolved sentient life-forms that would ultimately develop the extraordinary capacity for self-reflective awareness, simply in order for them to be able to experience happiness?

It's my conviction that we are here for a reason, that there is a grand and great purpose to our presence in this universe, and that none of us are going to truly find what we are looking for unless we get over our misguided pursuit of personal happiness and connect with that greater sense of purpose – that ultimate reason for being.

Each day has a spiritual quality, a special meaning inherent only in the state of mindfulness.

To awaken to the preponderance of oneness, to awaken to the integrity of harmony, to awaken to the completeness of unity – these are our ultimate reasons for being.

Such is the very evolution of all humankind.

In her newest fascinating work, spiritual author Michele Doucette delves into the nature of the universe, addressing the work findings of both physicist Alain Aspect and physicist David Bohm, which, together, seem to imply that the universe is a *gigantic and splendidly detailed hologram*, given that subatomic particles have been shown to be able to communicate with each other, regardless of the distance that separates them. Might this be the necessitated scientific proof that separateness is, and has always been, the illusion?

Their findings further suggest that every individual part of the hologram contains all of the information possessed by the whole. I found this particular insight to be a phenomenal leap into quantum physics; likewise, I also found it to be a fascinating piece of the puzzle in understanding the makeup of all matter. Not only does this apply to our physical makeup, as Michele points out, but it applies to our spiritual makeup as well.

If you consider, as Michele states, *that we are all sparks of the divine, that we are all offshoots of the same stem of consciousness* (God, my note), *it then becomes less challenging to grasp that, so, too, are we a hologram.*

She further quotes 18th century German philosopher, Immanuel Kant, who reached the startling conclusion that time and space are merely reflections of how the mind operates.

These remarkable insights, as denoted, including other deeper observations, are now believed and taught by modern researchers.

Neurophysiologist Karl Pribram believes that the brain itself is a hologram, which would explain how it can store so many memories in such a small space. Psychologist Keith Floyd has suggested that if our reality is a hologram, then it would no longer be true to say that the brain produces consciousness; instead, it is consciousness that creates the appearance of the brain, including the body and everything else, around us, that we interpret as being physical.

It is this supposition that leads one to an entirely new concept of reality.

Weaving these thoughts together, along with those of other great thinkers, Michele paints a clear picture of modern thought, one that shows how the nature of the universe and humanity are tied together by a great design.

In so doing, she also presents controversial healing techniques based on this remarkable philosophy, enabling the reader to envision a new reality, one that is hinged upon their individual ability as both creation and co-creator of the whole.

Building on the belief that each individual is a divine being, and the master of his or her own destiny, and that each action we take is based upon personal choices, she also makes us aware that these choices determine the degree of harmony and peace within our lives.

The power of the mind, as demonstrated in this book, is infinitely far greater than most have dared to imagine.

By consciously working to reconfigure our minds, we can free ourselves of the chatter within them, including the negativity around us, thereby achieving the peace and tranquility that already exists within.

In an effort to transcend the mind and ego, Michele outlines specific steps and ways to accomplish this goal, thereby enabling the reader to become awakened to the vitally alive *real* Self. It is this type of transformation that will change the life of each reader who puts these principles into action.

Throughout the text, Michele talks about spiritual science, lucid living, energy, vibration, the outer world being one's mirror, mindfulness, spiritual development, connecting to the now, soul transcendence, consciousness cleanse, coherence, polarity and oneness, while also referencing additional terms in relation to Gnosis, or Spiritual Wisdom.

She addresses the basic Cathari belief as having been one in which Jesus came to reveal truth as related to our eternal and spiritual essence, as opposed to redeeming mankind from sin.

In truth, the spiritual teachings of the Cathars were very similar to the actual teachings and examples of Jesus, both promoting love, tolerance, and equality between men and women.

Gnosticism places great emphasis on spiritual knowledge as compared to faith, through a mystical inner contemplative experience and acquaintance with the divine. Michele teaches that a study and practice of these principles, today, will bring about a new spiritual awakening.

She also highlights Zen Buddhism, a philosophy which teaches that without the attainment of satori, through individual personal experience, no one can enter into the truth of Zen. Attained through Zazen (or a cross-legged sitting practice), such provides release from all clinging, and therefore, from all suffering.

It is her belief that the current spiritual changes are bringing about *a revolution, not only in human thought, but in society as a whole*; meaning that this very change (one that steadfastly involves unconditional love and forgiveness), shall be the one that allows us to *embrace all things as they are*.

Directing the reader towards experiencing freedom, harmony and unity, on an inner level, is the intent of this work.

Stanley J. St. Clair, author of *Prayers of Prophets, Knights and Kings* and *Mysterious People of the Bible in the Light of History*

In this latest work, *The Awakening of Humanity: A Foremost Necessity*, you have been able to capture the essence of what this life journey is all about.

This is a book that everyone should have at their side; a book to remind one's self, from time to time, that life is what we make it. We are the producers and the actors; it is all up to us.

You have taken a very complex subject and successfully dissected it to its core.

Jean-Guy, Poirier, Canada

This book is a *must-read* for every seeker of Truth, whether they are on a quest for discovering the truths necessary to creating a better humanity for all, or whether they are on a personal journey to find the truths that lie within themselves.

Michele has shared, alongside her own profound insights, the writings of those who have taught and inspired her the most.

I was both treated to a wealth of amazing thoughts, from some of my favorite thinkers, as well as introduced to many new ones, all of which allowed me to grasp a better understanding of what may have shaped their lives and thinking, giving me an even greater respect for them and their individual contributions to our collective well-being.

While Michele's message is as positive, inspiring and as powerful as that of *The Secret*, it fluidly moves us even further beyond by emphasizing several key points: the necessity of being aware of the connectedness of each of us to one another and the importance of how our actions, toward ourselves and others, affect our own outcome in life. She explains that when manifesting the positive in our own lives, this is the way to honouring our responsibility in helping (guiding) others achieve the same.

I was also presented with new concepts that were then applied to understanding my own life, concepts that suddenly made sense to me, each seeming to fall in place like the pieces of an exquisite puzzle.

This is when I found myself both studying the words, and applying them, to paradoxes and old thought patterns that I have struggled with for so long.

In sharing the profound truths that are presented within, this gentle book reads like a love letter. This information, provided by Michele, allowed me to view, and apply, these truths with new understanding toward my own; it felt as if she had written this book just for me. No doubt, the same will hold true for every reader.

This book is a gift; may you, too, find your own gift within its pages.

Mariel Barney Hunkeler, Ghost PRO (Paranormal Research Organization)

In placing herself (as she once was) where many readers are now, Michele gently guides us along a path of wisdom and awakening toward healing; one that enables each to find peace and harmony within themselves.

This is an incredibly intuitive author, and, as always, I have come away, after reading another of Michele Doucette's uplifting books, feeling like I have learned so much, while also being reminded, in perfect timing, of the things I had forgotten. There was much here that I needed to learn, bringing into my awareness many things of great importance and absolute necessity.

As always, Michele has done so much research, drawing from nay well known and important sources; in fact, the bibliography alone will keep you reading for a very long time.

This author is one of the most dedicated researchers that I have the privilege to know. I greatly appreciated her sharing such insights as this quote from Osho ... *Awareness is the lamp* [that will disperse the darkness, my note]; *be a lamp unto yourself. Awareness is the greatest alchemy there is. Just go on becoming more and more aware, and you will find your life changing for the better in every possible dimension. It will bring great fulfillment.*

I also resonated with this quote from Andrew Cohen … *It's my conviction that we are here for a reason, that there is a grand and great purpose to our presence in this universe, and that none of us are going to truly find what we are looking for unless we get over our misguided pursuit of personal happiness and connect with that greater sense of purpose – that ultimate reason for being.*

As soon as I began reading, I was learning new things, with terms, with terms and concepts such as spiritual science, which Michele shares as being *a process whereby knowledge of the soul is derived from a systematic study of the things we perceive with our senses, including the intuition.*

Likewise, she has also included significant information from well known Physicists, Alain Aspect and David Bohm.

With the diverse information contained within, spiritual, scientific and otherwise, I find myself connecting most closely to terms and teachings that I have read before in many of her previous works.

The chapter on Mindfulness resonated so fully with me, that I found myself going over and over it in my mind after the reading. *While stilling the chatter of the mind can aid in mental and physical relaxation, what is even more important is recognizing and acknowledging that you are not your mind. Transcending the dualistic mind is the battle of surrendering the bullying of the mind (ego dominated existence) to mindfulness (awareness of one's thoughts, actions and motivations). Mindfulness means being aware of the moment in which we are living.*

I could go on and on, referencing quotes and pointing out more of these profound wisdoms, but then, I would only be taking away from your personal experience. In conclusion, there is only one way to benefit from such a wonderful author, and that is to purchase the book. As you find yourself being completely involved in all of your actions, within every moment, the reading of this book will be the greatest gift you can give yourself *and* humanity.

Suzi Cullen, Australia

The ultimate goal in life is to experience spiritual enlightenment, a conscious uniting of mind with soul. Far from being a casual Sunday stroll, this journey requires total dedication, discipline, knowledge and courage.

In the words of another truth seeker … "there is no fee at the gateway to the path leading to spiritual enlightenment. The key to enter is the burning desire to know the truth. You need no expensive spiritual enlightenment workshops or classes, gurus or teachers, correspondence courses, retreats, or trips to India on the path. You, the student, are your own teacher; you just need to realize the truth and apply it as you ascend the path. You are an individualized conscious part of the Whole; all knowledge is within your grasp." [1]

---

[1] *Spiritual Enlightenment Path of the Seeker* accessed on April 25, 2011 at http://www.seekeronline.org/

In the course of my research, I came across a term that was quite new to me ... spiritual science ... its definition being "a process whereby knowledge of the soul is derived from a systematic study of the things we perceive with our senses, including the intuition." [2]

Spiritual science (without doctrine as well as without scripture) is "the study of all religions and belief systems, taking from them the best that each has to offer. Spiritual science also includes the practice of meditation and constant observation of one's thoughts, words and deeds. It is a disciplined philosophical way of life," [3] a most conscious way of living.

Remembering that Plato wrote ... *philosophy is the greatest good which the gods have conferred upon men* ... it can be said, then, that one who studies philosophy is a lover of wisdom.

---

[2] *What is Spiritual Science?* Article accessed on April 25, 2011 at http://www.thesanctuarycongregation.org/HTML/whatis.html
[3] Ibid.

In continuation, those who study and practice spiritual science are "lovers of wisdom whose lives are devoted to the discovery and application of truth." [4]

Manly P. Hall, in <u>First Principles of Philosophy</u>, shares that by philosophy "we can live wisely and die well. Those who perfect themselves in wisdom are called twice-born, for by wisdom, man is given a new birth. He departs from the old life with its uncertainties and limitations into a new illumined existence. Love rules the sphere of the wise. Those who have learned to love life in its deepest and most mystical senses have escaped from bondage of fear and dwell in peace with all things." [5]

I am quickly discovering that spiritual science, as an open-ended system of thought, is one that "continually grows as humankind evolves, drawing on the frontiers of human knowledge as well as the wisdom of the ages." [6]

---

[4] *What is Spiritual Science?* Article accessed on April 25, 2011 at http://www.thesanctuarycongregation.org/HTML/whatis.html
[5] Ibid.
[6] Ibid.

Like myself, if you believe that each individual is a divine being; if you believe that each individual is the master of his or her destiny; if you believe that each individual is alone responsible for their thoughts, words, actions and deeds; if you believe that connecting with the stream of consciousness (unified field, oneness), to which we all adhere, is what determines the degree of harmony and peace of mind that ensues within; if you believe that each individual should be encouraged to think for themselves, thereby maintaining their own authentic power ... then, you, too, are a spiritual scientist.

There is no particular path that must be taken in order to become spiritually enlightened, for all paths lead back to the same inherent destination of self realization and self actualization.

When you come to understand that you are both creation, as well as co-creator, of this vast, majestic, infinite universe, this is when you will begin to understand, through outward expression, the unlimited potential that exists within each and every being.

We are here …….

to experience gnosis, a direct spiritual experiential and intuitive knowledge.

to experience satori, that flash of sudden awareness, or realization, of individual enlightenment.

to experience bodhi, an awakening experience akin to that attributed to Gautama Buddha.

to experience nirvana, the perfect peace, the perfect state of mind, the perfect state of compassion for all, while also being completely free from suffering as well as individual existence.

to experience kensho, the name for an enlightenment in which you realize the non-duality of both the observer (subject) and the observed (object), and are thereby able to see your true self.

to experience moksha, freedom from desire and other worldly passions.

In short, we are here to wake up and smell the coffee, as it were, because in so doing, we will have progressed from the beginning of ego development to the final stages of spiritual enlightenment; in essence, two parts of the same process.

During the early formation of what would later come to be known as Christianity, church authorities (deemed Fathers of the Church of Rome) exerted considerable influence (energy) in weeding out what they termed *false* doctrine.

The Cathars (stated to have been derived from the Greek word, *katharoi*, meaning pure ones), it is said, most emulated the Gnostics. While the writings of the Cathars have, for the most part, been destroyed (because of the doctrinal threat as perceived by the Papacy), there are a few texts that were preserved by their opponents.

The *Rituel Cathare de Lyon* provides us with a mere glimpse of the inner workings of their faith.

A Latin manuscript, *The Book of Two Principles*, kept in Florence, is "a translation made in 1260 from a work by the Cathar Jean de Lugio from Bergamo (written in 1230). The Latin translation, found in Prague in 1939, came from an anonymous treaty written in Languedoc at the beginning of the 13th century." [7] It is conceivable that the author may have been the Parfait Barthelemy of Carcassonne. This particular work outlines "the basis of a complete dualism that are reflected in a veiled way in the Holy Scriptures." [8]

In accordance with Cathari belief, Jesus came to transmit a message, to reveal the truth (as related to our real eternal and spiritual essence) and *not* to redeem the sins of all men by his death.

Likewise, the beliefs of the Cathars very much coincided with Jesus' example of life (through his teachings): "non-violence but pure love, rejection of using the evil or force to resist the evil, and holy will in responding to attacks of the evil only with sacrifice." [9]

Their message was one of love, tolerance, freedom and equality between men and women.

---

[7] The Books by Gilles C. H.Nullens accessed on April 25, 2011 at http://www.nullens.org/catholics-heretics-and-heresy/part-1-the-cathars/1-2-introduction-to-the-cathar-religion-2/
[8] *Cathar Church and Doctrine* article accessed on April 25, 2011 at http://lespiraldelconeixement.com/dossier.cfm?lang=en&id=42
[9] *Cathar Church and Doctrine* article accessed on April 25, 2011 at http://lespiraldelconeixement.com/dossier.cfm?id=44

The Gnostics placed emphasis on spiritual knowledge (gnosis) as compared to faith; a self-knowledge obtained through understanding, courtesy of an inner, mystical (or esoteric) and contemplative experience (whereby one acquires knowledge of, and acquaintance with, the divine), coupled with purified living (conscious living) in keeping with all life.

Likewise, satori, that flash of sudden awareness, or realization, of individual enlightenment, the spiritual goal of Zen Buddhism, can only be attained through personal experience. It has been stated that without the attainment of satori, "no one can enter into the truth of Zen." [10]

Although satori is "a consequence of Zazen (which refers to a Zen sitting practice), one is not to be attached to attaining satori, for satori is the exquisite release from all clinging

---

[10] *Satori in Zen Buddhism* article accessed on April 25, 2011 at http://sped2work.tripod.com/satori.html

and, therefore, from suffering. Satori is wisdom that penetrates to, and radiates from, the whole being." [11]

In Buddhism, bodhi refers to the awakening experience as attained by Gautama Buddha. Having reached bodhi, it is believed that one is freed from the cycle of birth, suffering, death and rebirth. Bodhi has also been referred to as enlightenment, when, in actual fact, it is more akin to the notion of awakening from a dream (illusion) and of being aware and knowing (reality). It is more accurate, then, to think of bodhi as a type of spiritual awakening (a merging of the human and the divine).

Bodhi is attained when "the ten fetters that bind a human being to the wheel of samsara have been dissolved; when the Four Noble Truths have been fully understood and all volitional conditioning has reached cessation (nirodha), giving rise to transcendent peace (nibbana)." [12]

---

[11] *How to Practice the Six Points of Zen Satori* article accessed on April 25, 2011 at http://www.ehow.com/how_4424251_practice-six-points-zen-satori.html
[12] http://en.wikipedia.org/wiki/Bodhi

Herein, volitional conditioning refers to a mental disposition that is formed, courtesy of one's choice (decision). The very moment that "the psychological roots of all greed (lobha), aversion (dosa), delusion (moha), ignorance (avijjā), craving (tanha) and ego-centered consciousness (attā) are completely uprooted," [13] one experiences transcendent peace.

The Pāli Tripiṭaka, the standard collection of scriptures, identifies the ten fetters as being ... [1] belief in an individual self, [2] doubt or uncertainty, especially about the teachings, [3] attachment to rites and rituals, [4] sensual desire, [5] ill will, [6] lust for material existence, [7] lust for immaterial existence, [8] pride in self, (conceit, arrogance), [9] restlessness, distraction, anxiety and [10] ignorance. [14]

The Noble Eightfold Path [15] is the fourth of Buddha's Four Noble Truths (which comprise the core of Buddhist teaching).

---

[13] http://en.wikipedia.org/wiki/Bodhi
[14] Ibid.
[15] http://www.thebigview.com/buddhism/eightfoldpath.html

The attainment of nirvana is also what "breaks the otherwise endless rebirth cycle of reincarnation." [16] Buddhists consider nirvana to be "freedom from all worldly concerns such as greed, hate, and ignorance." [17]

As is the case with all of these differing enlightenment based terms, nirvana cannot be described adequately in words; it can only be experienced directly.

While kensho and satori share the same meaning, the term satori implies a much deeper experience. Kensho, then, refers to "a general mental upheaval that destroys the old accumulations of intellection and lays down the foundation for new life." [18]

To experience moksha means that one experiences a release from such things as freedom from desire and other worldly passions; things that continue to keep one bound to the endless cycle of rebirth and reincarnation.

---

[16] *Nirvana* entry accessed on April 25, 2011 at
http://library.thinkquest.org/28505/buddhism/nirva.htm
[17] Ibid.
[18] *Kensho* article accessed on April 25, 2011 al http://the-wanderling.com/kensho.html

Clearly, there is much discipline needed in an attempt to cultivate mindfulness and wisdom. In order to attain wisdom (insight and understanding), one must begin by understanding the very nature of the universe.

In 1982, a research team situated at the University of Paris, lead by physicist Alain Aspect, discovered something rather extraordinary.

Aspect and his team were able to discern "that under certain circumstances subatomic particles such as electrons are able to instantaneously communicate with each other regardless of the distance separating them ... whether they are 10 feet or 10 billion miles apart." [19]

Based on Aspect's findings, physicist David Bohm, of the University of London, believes that the universe is a "gigantic and splendidly detailed hologram." [20]

Bohm believes the reason subatomic particles are able to remain in contact with one another, regardless of the distance separating them, is "not because they are sending

---

[19] Talbot, Michael. *The Universe as a Hologram* article accessed on Aril 28, 2011 at http://twm.co.nz/hologram.html
[20] Ibid.

some sort of mysterious signal back and forth, but because their separateness is an illusion. He argues that, at some deeper level of reality, such particles are not individual entities, but are actually extensions of the same fundamental something;" [21] meaning that every individual part of the hologram contains all of the information possessed by the whole.

If you consider that we are all sparks of the divine, that we are all offshoots of the same stream of consciousness, that we are all individuated aspects of the same (because we wanted to experience ourselves in all ways), and therefore harbor all of the information possessed by the whole, it becomes less challenging to grasp that so, too, are we a hologram.

It also means that at a deeper level of reality, everything (and everyone) contained within this vast universe is interconnected on an infinite level.

---

[21] Talbot, Michael. *The Universe as a Hologram* article accessed on Aril 28, 2011 at http://twm.co.nz/hologram.html

Long before modern science knew anything about the processes of perception or the structure of matter, there was an eighteenth-century German philosopher, by the name of Immanuel Kant, who had "drawn a clear distinction between our perception of reality and the actual object of perception. He argued that all we ever know is how reality appears to us." [22]

It was Kant's reasoning that "our experience is as much a reflection of the nature of the mind as it is of the physical world. This led him to one of his boldest, and, at the time, most astonishing, conclusions of all. *Time and space*, he argued, *are not inherent qualities of the physical world; they are a reflection of the way the mind operates. They are part of the perceptual framework within which our experience of the world is constructed.*" [23]

---

[22] Russell, Peter. *Reality and Consciousness: Turning the Superparadigm Inside Out* article accessed on Aril 28, 2011 at http://twm.co.nz/prussell.htm#Time
[23] Ibid.

As strange as Kant's proposal may have seemed in his own time, and strange as it may still seem to many living in the 21st century, contemporary science is now proving him right.

Bohm is not the only researcher who has found evidence that the universe is a hologram. Working independently, in the field of brain research, Karl Pribram, a neurophysiologist located at Stanford, "believes memories are encoded not in neurons, or small groupings of neurons, but in patterns of nerve impulses that crisscross the entire brain in the same way that patterns of laser light interference crisscross the entire area of a piece of film containing a holographic image." [24]

In short, Pribram believes the brain, itself, is a hologram, which also explains "how the human brain can store so many memories in so little space." [25]

---

[24] Talbot, Michael. *The Universe as a Hologram* article accessed on Aril 28, 2011 at http://twm.co.nz/hologram.html
[25] Ibid.

Having already determined that "holograms possess an astounding capacity for information storage," [26] it is this most astonishing fact that mirrors, and further enhances, Pribram's theory in that "our uncanny ability to quickly retrieve whatever information we need from the enormous store of our memories becomes more understandable if the brain functions according to holographic principles." [27]

However, this amazing storage of memory is "not the only neurophysiological puzzle that becomes more tractable in light of Pribram's holographic model of the brain. Another is how the brain is able to translate the avalanche of frequencies it receives via the senses (light frequencies, sound frequencies, and so on) into the concrete world of our perceptions. Just as a hologram functions as a sort of lens, a translating device able to convert an apparently meaningless blur of frequencies into a coherent image, Pribram believes the brain also comprises a lens and uses holographic principles to mathematically convert the frequencies it

---

[26] Talbot, Michael. *The Universe as a Hologram* article accessed on Aril 28, 2011 at http://twm.co.nz/hologram.html
[27] Ibid.

receives through the senses into the inner world of our perceptions." [28]

The most mind-boggling aspect of Pribram's holographic model of the brain, however, is what happens when it is put together with Bohm's theory.

If, indeed, "the concreteness of the world is but a secondary reality" [29] and if there is "actually a holographic blur of frequencies" [30] with the brain, acting as a hologram, only selecting "some of the frequencies out of this blur" [31] and mathematically transforming them into sensory perceptions, what, then, happens to objective reality?

Are you ready for the answer? It simply ceases to exist.

As the religions of the East have long upheld, "the material world is Maya, an illusion, and although we may think we are physical beings moving through a physical world, this,

---

[28] Talbot, Michael. *The Universe as a Hologram* article accessed on Aril 28, 2011 at http://twm.co.nz/hologram.html
[29] Ibid.
[30] Ibid.
[31] Ibid.

too, is an illusion. We are really *receivers* floating through a kaleidoscopic sea of frequency, and what we extract from this sea and transmogrify into physical reality is but one channel from many extracted out of the superhologram." [32]

This striking new picture of reality, the synthesis of both views, referencing Bohm as well as Pribram, is now known as the *holographic paradigm*.

Having been greeted with skepticism by many, so, too, has it served to galvanize others, with a small, but growing, group of researchers, believing that "it may be the most accurate model of reality science has arrived at thus far. Numerous researchers, including Bohm and Pribram, have noted that many para-psychological phenomena become much more understandable in terms of the holographic paradigm." [33]

In a universe "in which individual brains are actually indivisible portions of the greater hologram and everything

---

[32] Talbot, Michael. *The Universe as a Hologram* article accessed on Aril 28, 2011 at http://twm.co.nz/hologram.html
[33] Ibid.

is infinitely interconnected, telepathy may merely be the accessing of the holographic level." [34]

Stanislav Grof, a psychiatrist (with more than fifty years experience researching the healing and transformative potential of non-ordinary states of consciousness), feels that the holographic paradigm model offers a clear understanding for much "of the baffling phenomena experienced by individuals during altered states of consciousness." [35]

As Grof himself has noted, "if the mind is actually part of a continuum, a labyrinth that is connected not only to every other mind that exists or has existed, but to every atom, organism, and region in the vastness of space and time itself, the fact that it is able to occasionally make forays into the labyrinth and have transpersonal experiences no longer seems so strange." [36]

---

[34] Talbot, Michael. *The Universe as a Hologram* article accessed on Aril 28, 2011 at http://twm.co.nz/hologram.html
[35] Ibid.
[36] Ibid.

Keith Floyd, a psychologist at Virginia Intermont College, has pointed out that "if the concreteness of reality is but a holographic illusion, it would no longer be true to say the brain produces consciousness. Rather, it is consciousness that creates the appearance of the brain, as well as the body and everything else around us we interpret as physical." [37]

The implications of this are equally amazing.

What we view as miraculous remissions of disease "may actually be due to changes in consciousness, which, in turn, effect changes in the hologram of the body." [38]

Similarly, this also means that "controversial new healing techniques, such as visualization, may work well because, in the holographic domain of thought, images are ultimately as real as reality." [39]

---

[37] Talbot, Michael. *The Universe as a Hologram* article accessed on Aril 28, 2011 at http://twm.co.nz/hologram.html
[38] Ibid.
[39] Ibid.

What we perceive as reality, therefore, is only a blank canvas, meaning that we are free to envision upon it any picture we want; hence, anything is possible.

As Pribram has pointed out, "even random events would have to be seen as based on holographic principles and therefore determined. Synchronicities, or meaningful coincidences, suddenly make sense, and everything in reality would have to be seen as a metaphor, for even the most haphazard events would express some underlying symmetry." [40]

Now that I have given everyone, myself included, something to think about (which, in truth, is just the tip if the iceberg), let us continue to proceed.

---

[40] Talbot, Michael. *The Universe as a Hologram* article accessed on Aril 28, 2011 at http://twm.co.nz/hologram.html

You are both co-creator, as well as creation, of this vast, majestic, infinite universe.

Everything is created within your own consciousness.

Everything created by you has first existed in thought, followed by feeling. Knowing that the thought, then, materializes into your external reality, it becomes important to become increasingly aware of what you are thinking.

Most people are *enslaved by their thoughts*, thereby *creating by default* (creation by way of an unconscious means).

It simply does not occur to them that they can free themselves from the chatter of the mind.

There can be no peace of mind, no stillness, when one is engulfed by negativity, and, yet, inner peace is within reach of each and every individual.

Therein lies the juxtaposition, if you will.

When the mind is silent, happiness reigns inside and out. It is to one's advantage, therefore, to be able to still the incessant and compulsive chatter of the mind.

The majority are so deeply ingrained within the confines of the human race that they often defer their thinking to someone other than themselves.

Everyday life, for the multitude, seems to be fraught with worry, tension, anxiety and fear. Thoughts arise in the mind, then, that also serve to reflect these same outer feelings.

In order to break free (so as to regain control of their own mind), one first has to become aware of the problem. Thereafter, one must work, consciously and diligently, toward reconfiguring how one thinks, how one responds, how one acts.

The source of all thought is, of course, the conscious mind; the segment that also deals with logic, reasoning (inductive, deductive, analytic and synthetic) and judgment.

The source of all power, on the other hand, is the subconscious mind; the segment that deals with intuition, emotion, inspiration, memory and imagination.

You must learn to *think only about what you want*, accepting it as part of your life.

It is also imperative that you achieve vibrational harmony with what you are creating.

You will know that you have achieved, and/or are achieving, alignment with your thought(s) when you feel happy, contented, elated, peaceful, ecstatic, overjoyed, playful and upbeat.

The deeper the feeling(s) experienced, the closer the alignment.

The power of expectation is key.

Expectation is intention.

Likewise, thought is also intention.

If "you desire one thing while expecting another, you are sending out two intentions that conflict and oppose each other; to be completely intentional, it means you [must] think about your desire and expect it to happen. Having all your thoughts in alignment with a single direction will ensure that your desire manifests without complications." [41] Knowing what you want gives you that clarity.

Repetition of a chant, a mantra, an affirmation ... all leads to belief. As soon as the belief has become instilled as a deep conviction, things begin to happen. Therein lies the psychology, and power, of repeated suggestion (which can also be used wrongly, so please be careful in this respect).

Fearful thoughts create fearful situations and hard times. By direct association, when all of the citizens of this planet stop thinking about war and destruction, so, too, will these perils depart.

We create by way of our emotional thinking.

---

[41] Tan, Enoch. *Power of Expectation* article (August 2008).

Thought is the greatest force in the world, and, as stated earlier, *everything begins with thought*. Whatever you fix your thought(s) upon (meaning whatever you steadily fix your imagination on) is what you shall attract.

It is imperative that you work to keep your dynamic vision alive, without being swayed by what you read, by what you see, by what you hear. Pictures (as in vision boards) can be very instrumental. The more often you visualize your desire, the faster its manifestation shall be.

It is a known scientific fact that, relative to quantum cohabitation, two atoms (mass) cannot occupy the same quantum space simultaneously. This is referred to as the Pauli-Einstein principle.

If you keep your mind filled with positive, creative and powerful thoughts, there will be little space left for that which is negative (fearful, doubtful and troublesome).

You must decide which thoughts shall continue to reside within your own mind.

As individuals think and believe, this is what they become. Every person is an image of their own thinking and believing.

It must also be reiterated that the subconscious automatically responds to the thoughts that dominate.

Unless you successfully close your mind to negative thoughts, counteracting them with positive ones, sooner or later even the most powerful will succumb to the destructive effects of these negative thoughts.

A mental picture is the same thing as a thought projection; just envision the movie projectors of old in order to achieve an operable visual. If these thought projections remain steadfast and unwavering, it is with consistent practice and concentrated effort that you achieve that which you desire, all courtesy of the subconscious mind. In short, you become energized action in motion.

The more interest you take in any initiative, the more attention and energy you naturally give.

Knowing that energy follows thought, it only makes sense that you continue to experience greater results in keeping with said initiative; the more absorbing the initiative, the better.

Possessing the right mental attitude, in combination with remaining firmly fixed on that which is your steadfast goal, is what creates the necessary ambiance to achieve.

It becomes through the cooperation of both the conscious and subconscious mind that all can succeed.

All must believe (earnestly, sincerely, strongly and completely), for it is belief that makes things happen.

Knowing that many continue to be controlled by way of collective (mass) thinking, true happiness, as sought by many, has always been actualized by so few.

Located within, happiness is a state of mind that we, ourselves, have the power to control.

When you come to know yourself (completely and in all ways) while also taking full ownership and responsibility for that which you create, you will also come to know (and wholeheartedly embrace) the power of thought.

Just take the time to think about using your power to develop a healthy, caring and open minded outlook towards the interconnectedness of life (demonstrating empathy for others, demonstrating an important life purpose, seeking a balance between work, play, creativity and spirituality); all of which serves to create a healthy body.

Most have experienced that special, almost magical, moment in which everything seems perfect.

Each time I am holding a sleeping newborn, I feel the completeness, the wholeness, the perfection, of life. Likewise, I also experience them when held in a warm embrace by someone who loves me. When I am engaged in a writing project, one that requires extensive research as well as personal reflection, so, too, am I able to tap into these same, wondrous, energies.

These are the moments of oneness with creation. You feel a sense of rightness, a sense of innate goodness.

These are the very moments that restore us spiritually.

These are the very moments that recharge us emotionally.

These are the very moments that do wonders for us on a physical level, making us feel more vibrant and alive.

You have the power to experience these moments each day, should that be your wish.

To transcend the mind is akin to watching your thoughts and feelings pass by, choosing which thought and/or feeling to entertain at any given moment.

While stilling the chatter of the mind can aid in mental and physical relaxation, what is even more important is recognizing and acknowledging that you are not your mind.

Transcending the dualistic mind is the battle of surrendering the bullying of the mind (ego dominated existence) to mindfulness (awareness of one's thoughts, actions and motivations).

Mindfulness means being aware of the moment in which we are living.

Mindfulness is meditation in action, allowing life to unfold without the limitation of prejudgment.

Mindfulness means being open to awareness whilst becoming the *Infinite Possibilitarian* that author Norman Vincent Peale addresses in his work.

Mindfulness pertains to existing in a relaxed state of attentiveness, one that involves both the inner world of thoughts and feelings, as well as the outer world of actions and perceptions.

Choosing at least one activity each day, to carry out in a mindful manner (giving it your full attention), helps considerably.

If you are chopping vegetables, take the time to absorb the colors, the textures, the smells, the motions, the tastes.

If you are exercising on a treadmill, take the time to feel your muscles moving as you walk, run, jog, speed up, slow down.

That having been said, one can learn to live the entirety of their day in mindful meditation.

There is no witness. There is no judgment. You have succeeded in becoming an observer without engaging the mind.

Thoughts and feelings are simply thoughts and feelings. They are not who you are.

Before one can work toward transcending the mind, one must reprogram (reconfigure) the subconscious mind.

This is what I had to do in order to eclipse a life filled with total negative media bombardment.

Meditation is but one avenue open to the seeker.

At first, you will hear your own thoughts forming in your mind. You may quickly come to realize that there tends to be much continuous repetition to your thoughts.

Herein lies the greatest challenge, for there will be many thoughts that will arise as you are attempting to meditate.

In the very beginning, you will find yourself getting lost in them. Trying to remain unattached to the chatter in your head is the most difficult part.

You merely wish to become an observer, standing at the sidelines, if you will. As soon as you pass judgment on what you are observing, the thoughts will drag you down.

Pretend that you are outside, observing the clouds as they float across the sky. Now imagine your thought forms as the very clouds that are passing you by.

It is in coming to this realization that you can honestly say *I have become a witness to my own mind.*

There may also be pictures and images that begin to filter through. Try to become a witness to these visualizations as well.

Do not engage with either the thoughts or the images. Simply accept them while remaining unattached. Do not judge them. Remember, you are merely the observer.

You may also notice your body responding (emotional reactions) to specific thought forms that are filtering through. Once again, you must step out of the emotion.

One should not allow an emotion to control them while in the physical body. You are merely the observer. You may continue to be the witness, but only without judgment.

Even though *becoming a witness* to thought forms, pictures, images and emotions, is not an easy task, it is something that *needs to be practiced every day*.

As you are able to experience success with this while in a meditative state, so, too, shall you be able to practice *living a waking meditation* throughout your entire day.

While it is imperative that you become aware of what goes on in your mind when you are going about your daily life, it is important that you continue to step back, thereby maintaining the stance of an objective observer.

When you are able to experience this with considerable success, you can say that you are practicing a mindfulness type of meditation.

It is also important to realize that there is a monumental difference between you (as the observer) and the things that are observed by you.

As you become more of a witness to your own mind, your consciousness is becoming more aware of itself.

What this means is that the egoic mind will begin to become quiet so that you can learn to reside, in a pure and nonjudgmental way, in what can be called the *real* Self.

All of the varied forms of meditation have but one purpose: to introduce you to the experiencing of consciousness. With this, then, comes the realization that this is all there is.

As you dedicate yourself to this practice, on an intense and daily basis, you will begin to observe transformation on many levels, each as unique as the individual.

In addition to meditation, affirmations and visualizations can also be used as transformational tools, a way of bypassing the conscious mind.

Affirmations are personal statements written in both positive and present tense terms. The more emotion one evokes upon saying these affirmations aloud, the more powerful they become.

When it comes to visualization, yet another medium, I find it incredibly difficult to see the pictures while also trying to put myself in the image. It is quite difficult to get emotionally excited about a specific impression when all my mind sees are some dark and fuzzy attempts at a new reality.

Now that I have discovered Mind Movies,[42] an absolutely phenomenal metaphysical tool, I am able to visualize with increasing clarity. Mind Movies is a *multi-media tool* that allows you to create a vision of what you want, scored with your favorite song; the one that makes you feel good, the one that makes you want to dance, the one that makes you smile and sing along.

Freedom experienced on an inner level is the very freedom that all seek, for it is the *real freedom*. This is what you experience when you are able to still the mind.

A calm mind is a powerful mind.

---

[42] http://www.mindmovies.com/?10107

Peace, contentment, happiness and bliss are to be found when one experiences this silence, this stillness, this sense of calm.

Accordingly, there are also additional benefits.

You will find that your ability to concentrate improves.

You will find that you have more patience, showing more tact in responding to difficult situations.

You will find that others do not hold as much sway over you (what they think of you and say about you) as before.

You will find yourself responding to situations with less anxiety and worry.

As difficulties arise, you will demonstrate an increased ability to maintain a sense of inner poise and common sense.

You will find that you are sleeping better.

In addition, all of the above vastly improves your ability to meditate.

Inner peace enables one to feel grounded, to feel balanced. In these stressful times, this is what is needed by all.

Developing the ability to still the mind will take you a considerable distance towards attaining *and* maintaining inner balance and peace of mind.

Many are familiar with the term lucid dreaming, a term coined by Dutch psychiatrist and writer Frederik (Willem) van Eeden (1860 – 1932).

A lucid dream is a dream in which one is fully aware that they are dreaming. A lucid dream can begin in one of two ways: [1] a dream-initiated lucid dream (DILD) starts as a normal dream, and the dreamer eventually concludes it is a dream, while [2] a wake-initiated lucid dream (WILD) occurs when the dreamer goes from a normal waking state directly into a dream state, with no apparent lapse in consciousness. [43]

I have come across the term *lucid living* as used by author and philosopher Timothy Freke, whereby it references experiencing an ultra-awake state (lucid living); a state in which you are fully conscious that life is like a dream, [44]

[43] http://en.wikipedia.org/wiki/Lucid_Dreaming
[44] Freke, Timothy. (2005) *Lucid Living* (page 11). Carlsbad, CA: Hay House, Inc.

albeit the most magnificent, glorious, wonderful, intimate, diverse, and yet complex, vision.

Freke leads the reader through seven powerful insights that "work together to wake you up from the sleeping sickness that keeps you unconscious in the life-dream." [45]

[1] Life is a mystery.

I think that most would agree with this point. To a great many, life is completely unfathomable – hard to believe and difficult to understand. As Freke puts it, "life is the mother of all mysteries." [46]

Unless one has awakened to the now, life seems endless in the most dismal (dreary, gloomy, boring) of ways. In truth, life is *conscious* (fully aware, deliberate and intentional), life is *infinite* (boundless and endless), life is remarkable.

[2] Now is all you know.

---

[45] Freke, Timothy. (2005) *Lucid Living* (page 15). Carlsbad, CA: Hay House, Inc.
[46] Ibid, page 23.

What you experience in the now constitutes your truth.

It is essential, then, that you take the time to "examine your own immediate experience of living." [47]

[3] You are not a person.

This particular insight may be a tad confusing for some. However, when you consider that we are all sparks of the divine, that we are all offshoots of the same stream of consciousness, that we are all individuated aspects of the same (because we wanted to experience ourselves in all ways), it becomes less challenging to grasp.

Freke describes all of us as being an "experiencer of experiences," [48] which is exactly what happens when you become mindful enough to become both detached observer as well as witness to the role that you have temporarily embraced.

---

[47] Freke, Timothy. (2005) *Lucid Living* (page 38). Carlsbad, CA: Hay House, Inc.
[48] Ibid, page 46.

If you want to experience lucid living, you need to "stop believing that you are the person you appear to be right now" [49] so that you may "be awareness witnessing this ever-changing moment," [50] which, in reality, is who you really are.

[4] The world exists in you.

Once you are aware of the fact that what you feel, believe and demonstrate on the inside (courtesy of your thoughts, words, actions and deeds) is what shows up on the outside (the world as you know it), this is not an overly difficult concept to grasp.

As you become more conscious of who you are, in reality, the world you "experience" exists within your own consciousness, your own awareness.

[5] All is one.

---

[49] Freke, Timothy. (2005) *Lucid Living* (page 51). Carlsbad, CA: Hay House, Inc.
[50] Ibid.

When you consider that we are all sparks of the divine, that we are all offshoots of the same stream of consciousness, that we are all individuated aspects of the same (because we wanted to experience ourselves in all ways), clearly, we are all one, for therein lies the deep connection that we share.

As Freke puts it, we are "one awareness, dreaming itself to be many different personas in the life-dream," [51] meaning that we are "one awareness experiencing the life-dream from the different perspectives of these different personas." [52]

[6] You are a paradox.

Having learned that you are both the source of the dream as well as a character within the dream being dreamed, this is what makes each of us a paradox, does it not?

I find this particular insight to be most illuminating because I never thought of myself as being a paradox until the reading of Lucid Living.

---

[51] Freke, Timothy. (2005) *Lucid Living* (page 69). Carlsbad, CA: Hay House, Inc.
[52] Ibid.

This also means that as long as "you identify exclusively with your life-persona, you will remain unconsciously engrossed in the life-dream." [53]

Breaking out of the paradoxical box, then, is what leads to lucid living.

[7] Being one is loving all.

This insight relates to experiencing love for all life, for all creation, without limits.

In summation, lucid living does not equate to "believing the theory that life is like a dream. It is directly experiencing the dreamlike nature of reality in this present moment." [54]

Lucid Living by Timothy Freke is a book that asks you to partake of a philosophical experiment, one that examines the human predicament. Some may be ready, others not.

Are you?

---

[53] Freke, Timothy. (2005) *Lucid Living* (page 75). Carlsbad, CA: Hay House, Inc.
[54] Ibid, page 41.

Everything is comprised of energy. Everything is vibration. All vibration is the result of energy in motion. Energy is held together to create matter. Matter is energy condensed to a slow vibration.

There is one underlying field of energy, the unified field (also referred to as the Zero Point Field or ZPF), that pervades everything, thereby giving purpose and unity to our world.

Everything in the universe has a unique vibrational energy. Every object, every being, every thought, every action, every psychological mood; in short, energy equals vibration.

The quality of your vibratory signature depends on both your thoughts and your inner mental (feeling) world.

If one feels inadequate, insecure and lacking in self esteem, this results in an inward withdrawal.

These individuals tend to become engulfed in a negative inner dialogue, one that is embodied by self-pity.

It is this very negative vibration that emanates outward. In accordance with the Law of Attraction, this negative energy will only attract more of the same.

No matter how much this person seeks happiness and success, in their life, they continue to feel more and more like a dismal failure, at anything and everything.

They may not understand that it is one's inner world that must ultimately be changed before such can be duly reflected in the outer world of which they are a part.

Focus and concentration are major keys with respect to the changing of one's inner world.

It is your energy vibration that attracts corresponding circumstances (be they people, places, things or events) into your life.

By the same token, it is your energy vibration that can ultimately change your reality.

You are constantly projecting thought patterns.

If you are *conscious* of your thought patterns, then you are *creating by deliberate intent.*

If you are *unconscious* of your thought patterns, then you are *creating by default.*

The more you are able to remain open to a given experience, relaxing and embracing the situation at hand, doing your best to learn from the event itself, the easier it becomes to transcend, thereby allowing you to move beyond the experience in question.

Whatever you resist will persist, as the saying goes. It was Carl Jung who uttered these wise words. He was a man who clearly understood that what you think about recreates itself within your own life experience(s).

Negative energies, then, will only begin to dissipate in the welcoming, accepting and embracing of that which you want to change.

Most are familiar with the saying that *the outer world is your mirror*, always *reflecting yourself back to you*. This simply means that your outer world is a direct reflection of your inner world.

If you embrace and feel love, peace, unison and truth, vibrating such throughout the entirety of your being, you will experience people (as well as places, things or events) that reflect the same.

If, on the other hand, all you experience in your outer world is disharmony, aggression, hate, separation and falsehood, you will experience people (as well as places, things or events) that reflect the same.

Much inner healing is needed in order to correct the imbalances that exist.

Accepting the premise that you, and you alone, are 100% responsible for the changes that you wish to impart upon your being, is also critical.

I am here to tell you that it is possible to transcend situations in your outer world, all through *the shifting of your inner terrain.*

However, this is not something that happens overnight. It *is a process that requires work, effort and diligence* on your part, of that you can be sure.

While it is not known to whom the following quote can be attributed, it is well worth citing herein.

The good you find in others, is within you as well. The faults you find in others, are your faults as well. After all, to recognize something in your outer world, you must have a reference point in your inner world. The world around you is a reflection, a mirror showing you the person you are. To change your world, simply change yourself. See the best in others, and you will be at your best. Give to others, and you give to yourself. Love others, and you will be loved. Seek to understand, and you will be understood. Listen, and your voice will be heard. Teach, and you will learn.

Einstein's formula of E=MC² simply means that the mass of an object is multiplied by the speed of light squared.

The "speed of light is 186,282.397 miles per second, or 1,079,252,848.8 km per hour, which means that even in a relatively small amount of mass there is an enormous amount of inherent energy." [55]

Consciousness, like matter, is also a form of energy.

The transcendental state "is what you are encoded to be in your ultimate expressions of beingness. It is reliably imprinted upon your genetic code and is there for you to access when you choose to do so. These transcendental states will be your most natural level of expression; the one that feels most comfortable to you is where you find the realization of your greatest potential." [56]

---

[55] *Pathways of Transcendence* article accessed on April 20, 2011 at http://www.spiritheart.org/members/messages/07_08-22_pathways_of_transcendence.htm

[56] Ibid.

Living in the now refers to living in the moment. Living in the moment is also called mindfulness. In truth, nothing exists outside of this present moment.

As you become mindful of your thoughts, words, emotions, feelings and actions, you are learning to be fully present in the moment.

Whenever I find myself stressed, worried, angry or anxious, I stop what I am doing. I simply close my eyes and breathe.

Taking a deep breath, I hold it for a count of ten before slowing exhaling. I take the time to continue breathing, in this same manner, for several moments.

Many are controlled by their thoughts of stress, worry and anger. In order to feel more in control, you need to step out of, and learn to detach yourself from, that mode of existence, otherwise you shall never be able to locate the necessary pause in keeping with the now.

In coming to grips with the fact that you are not your thoughts, you eventually learn to become an observer of your thoughts (emotions, feelings) from moment to moment, without judging them.

You are here to awaken to experience.

You are here to live fully and completely.

You are here to enjoy life.

You are here to experience inner freedom.

You are here to live a life of empowerment.

If you are to experience anything in life, you must create it in the present moment because unless it exists in some form, in the here and now, it will not exist at all.

What is it, then, that you wish to create?

How do you feel about your life in this moment?

There is a considerable difference between creating freedom, peace, love, joy and wealth for yourself versus creating confinement, war, hatred, obligation and scarcity.

All that you wish for in the future (which refers to tomorrow) must be seeded in the here and now.

In the words of Andrew Cohen, editor of EnlightenNext Magazine ... *Spiritual development, as I understand it, is about compelling ourselves, through the power of our own inspired will and intention, to actually evolve. And in order to evolve, to consciously evolve, you first need to get to know the multidimensional nature of who you are and how you are. You need to be able to recognize and understand what constitutes your interior world — the infinite nature of the spiritual ground of your own being, the higher human capacities that make conscious evolution possible, and also the unconscious conditioned structures that can obstruct and obscure that potential. You need to examine the fundamental dimensions of the self, both relative and absolute; understand the unique challenges and potentials of the cultural context in which we find ourselves; and cultivate those higher human capacities that can enable you to participate in such a bold and significant task as the evolution of the interior of the cosmos.*

Like a great many held captive to their thoughts, to their feelings, to their emotions, I did not always live in the present moment.

I was so controlled by them that I was drowning in sorrow, depression, anxiety, worry and frustration. Instead of living, I was simply existing; there is little joy to be found within life choice.

You are not here to change anyone other than yourself. Translated another way, this means that you are here to live your own life.

How, then, must one live in order to make that much needed connection to the now?

[1] Take the time to reconnect with nature. Take the time to pay close attention to the sights, sounds, smells and textures (as in walking barefoot on both the dewy grass as well as the warm sand) that instantly rise up to greet you.

[2] Take the time to savour your food, enjoying their colors, textures, smells and taste combinations.

[3] Begin each day with the same routine (by greeting the sun as it rises high in the skyline; by engaging in meditation; by engaging in some form of exercise; by watching your Mind Movie; by perusing your vision board), unique to you and your needs.

[4] Engage in activities that both interest and excite you, fueling you with much needed energy (which translates to living your bliss). Take the time to do the things that you love.

[5] Stop playing video games in order to better engage your mind (books, crossword puzzles, movies).

[6] Take the time to focus on the things that really matter.

[7] Learn to become more positive (through identifying negative thoughts and mindsets and then reconfiguring them) each and every day.

[8] Take the time to feel the pain of suffering (as it comes your way) and then move forward, fully embracing all of the good that life has to offer.

[9] Take the time to truly understand the life of another (preferably someone living in conditions that are less than your own).

[10] Engage in play activities with children. More than anyone else, children know how to live in the moment. Take the time to relearn how to be joyful in your play with children and with each other.

[11] Recognize the importance of experiencing wisdom when you speak with your elders.

[12] Take the time to learn something new, to experience something that you have always wanted to experience.

[13] Rediscover your own spirituality.

[14] Take the time to learn to be still (while also relishing the stillness) by reading, sitting in the warm sun (and appreciating the warmth) or taking a nap.

[15] Stop watching the news on TV in order to learn to think for yourself, in order to learn to approach life from both a heart-based consciousness as well as a positive mindset.

[16] Rediscover comedy in all of its glorious forms; in truth, laughter is the best medicine.

In the words of Babatunde Olatunji ... *Yesterday is history. Tomorrow is a mystery. Today is a gift. That's why we call it the present.*

Transcendence pertains to being free from limitations inherent in matter, while also having continuous existence above and beyond the created world.

Simply put, transcendence means the real self, the fully conscious self, the essence of who and what you really are. Likewise, transcendence is also a self-mastery process that enables you to understand the differences between creating by conscious intent versus creating by default.

Transcendence pertains to living from a heart-based consciousness (love) instead of an ego-based consciousness (fear, guilt, power, control).

There are many different aspects that, in totality, add up to the definition of transcendence as shared herein.

[1] You must learn how to control your emotional responses, instead of the other way around, for the simple reason that as long as you are being controlled, you are not in control.

[2] You must learn to recognize the negative (thoughts, feelings, emotions, beliefs) that dwells within, replacing all with positive.

[3] You must learn to become an observer (to your thoughts, feelings, emotions) instead of a reactor.

[4] You must understand what balance means, applying this knowledge to your life on a daily basis.

[5] You must continue to see the all-encompassing picture (shared consciousness) as you strive to acknowledge, and work toward, the greater good in your life.

[6] Upon experiencing a profound modification of self, you must remain committed to living the new life experience(s).

To put it simply: *to know something, you must become it.*

In the words of John Roger, founder of the Movement of Spiritual Inner Awareness (MSIA) ... *All that you want to be, you already are. All you have to do is move your awareness there and recognize the reality of your own Soul.*

"The purpose of The Movement of Spiritual Inner Awareness (MSIA) is to teach Soul Transcendence, which is becoming aware of yourself as a Soul and as one with God, not as a theory but as a living reality. Your Soul is who you truly are; it is more than your body, your thoughts, or your feelings. It is the highest aspect of yourself, where you and God are one." [57]

Knowing that there is much joy and beauty in life, what is it that is keeping you from discovering this inner peace, this joy, this beauty, this total contentment?

Let's face it, we only have ourselves to blame when we worry and are fearful.

If we were to embrace any given situation with the calm acceptance (without complaint, without a grudge, without surrendering or giving up) of truth, simply allowing the body to go with the flow (because it is what it is), we would have transcended the illusionary world of ego eons ago.

---

[57] http://www.msia.org/soultranscendence

According to Debbie Ford, author of <u>The 21 Day Consciousness Cleanse: A Breakthrough Program for Connecting with Your Soul's Deepest Purpose</u>, transcendence involves stepping "into the enormity of what's possible for your life" [58] so that you may "live in the expansiveness of your future." [59]

There exists a simultaneous feeling, one that has often been described as "self-consciousness watching consciousness and consciousness arising as self-consciousness" [60] with no separation between the two, meaning that being human allows one to "be self-consciousness while swimming in the bliss of consciousness." [61]

---

[58] *Consciousness Cleanse Day 18 – The Light of Transcendence* article accessed on April 15, 2011 at
http://www.oprah.com/spirit/Consciousness-Cleanse-Day-18-The-Light-of-Transcendence
[59] Ibid.
[60] *Cosmic soup: The zero point field, transcendence-immanence, self-conscious consciousness and what was/is before words were/are?* article accessed on April 15, 2011 at
http://integrallife.com/member/ani-kowal/blog/cosmic-soup-zero-point-field-transcendence-immanence-self-conscious-consciousn
[61] Ibid.

As your mind completely transcends thought, you experience a state of restful alertness and inner peace.

This is what continues to be referred to as Transcendental Consciousness.

It has been said that the enlightened mind can attain and gain the true, transcendent type of free will, but only by emphatically rejecting the false, deluded type of free will. [62]

In knowing that everything, and everyone, is made of the same stuff, that all is a stream of consciousness, so, too, can consciousness be expressed in material (physical) form; while these forms may appear to be separate and distinct, this is not the case at all.

Our scientists have been able to observe that the entire universe is continually expanding, and at an accelerated rate. What, then, is it that drives this pace?

---

[62] *Transcending Determinism: Transcendent Freedom vs. Naïve Freewill Thinking* article accessed on April 19, 2011 at http://www.egodeath.com/TranscendingDeterminismVsNaiveFreewill.htm

It certainly "cannot be a material force, for no such force exists. And thus, the only rational, logical explanation is indeed that the real force that drives the universe is the fact that the universe is a stream of consciousness." [63]

Taking it one step further, "matter cannot transcend itself; matter cannot go beyond the state in which it was created. Yet consciousness has this ability, consciousness can reinvent itself, consciousness can transcend itself, consciousness can choose to let the old die and be reborn and be resurrected into a higher state." [64]

Just as the entire material universe is expanding at this ever accelerating rate, so, too, are you, as an individual, being "compelled by the very life force itself to expand your consciousness, in order keep up with what is happening to the universe." [65]

---

[63] *The Stream of Consciousness* article accessed on April 19, 2011 at http://quantumunlimited.org/vem/articles-english-mainmenu-82/1599-the-stream-of-consciousness

[64] Ibid.

[65] Ibid.

This expansion of consciousness "is what drives the material universe, the physical planets and galaxies, to move away from each other at an accelerated speed. The inhabitants of Earth are not expanding their state of consciousness at that rate; they are expanding it at a slower rate. And this means that the Earth is lagging behind the position in absolute space where it would have been, if it had followed the expansion rate of the universe as a whole." [66]

It is this lagging behind that creates the illusion of time as well as the "friction that creates so many problems on Earth that seem to have no solution. The reality is that the Earth is being pulled by the background expanding force of the universe to move through space at an ever increasing speed." [67]

In order "for the Earth to grow, there would have to be an ever increasing force [to resist the increased friction], and this is indeed what is currently the case. But there is an

---

[66] *The Stream of Consciousness* article accessed on April 19, 2011 at http://quantumunlimited.org/vem/articles-english-mainmenu-82/1599-the-stream-of-consciousness
[67] Ibid.

alternative to this scenario, for the ever-increasing force is necessary only to propel a body of the same density. "[68]

Here is an interesting scenario for you.

If the Earth was "becoming less and less dense, so that it was propelled to move faster" [69] because there was less friction and less resistance, this could also mean that the Earth would be able to "effortlessly move through space at an accelerated speed without there being an increase in force." [70]

In reality, what makes this plausibility even remotely possible is the acceleration of consciousness, whereby you "let go of the old sense of identity that was at a certain level of density ... [knowing that] when this happens on a collective scale, by all of humankind raising the collective consciousness, then the entire planet will become less

---

[68] *The Stream of Consciousness* article accessed on April 19, 2011 at http://quantumunlimited.org/vem/articles-english-mainmenu-82/1599-the-stream-of-consciousness
[69] Ibid.
[70] Ibid.

dense" [71] which means it can then "move through space at an ever accelerated pace without the application of greater and greater force," [72] for this is what shall bring about a revolution, not only in human thought, but in society as a whole.

There will no longer be a need for this "physical, mental, emotional force to keep the old structures alive" [73] for they will have been "replaced, not by new structures, but by the willingness to flow with the stream of life ... for you do not gain any longer your sense of identity from the structure, you gain it from seeing beyond structure, beyond even the structure of the Earth itself." [74]

Jean-Paul Sartre was the author of an essay, written in 1937, called The Transcendence of the Ego. Sartre refers to the fact that intentional objects are objects of consciousness, with their inherent value being their very consciousness.

---

[71] *The Stream of Consciousness* article accessed on April 19, 2011 at http://quantumunlimited.org/vem/articles-english-mainmenu-82/1599-the-stream-of-consciousness
[72] Ibid.
[73] Ibid.
[74] Ibid.

As we are conscious of things, so, too, are we also "conscious of ourselves being conscious of things," [75] meaning that "things and our own consciousness of the things, both evoke our own reflective consciousness." [76]

According to Sartre, the ego pertains to the states and actions that it supports, which is to say that "the material presence of things in turn proves the ontology of the object contemplating them. Ego is then nothing without something in which to contemplate, but is reliant on itself and its being; further, the flexibility of consciousness, for Sartre, is the ability to contemplate something in its absence," [77] which appears to be his idea of reflection.

Sartre concludes that while people are able to contemplate the same thing, we simply cannot comprehend the intuitive apprehension of another, which means we are only able to perceive (experience) that we are responsible for our own doings.

---

[75] http://en.wikipedia.org/wiki/The_Transcendence_of_the_Ego
[76] Ibid.
[77] Ibid.

In addition, while we are able to reflect on our own consciousness (of something), we are unable to reflect on the consciousness of another (of that same thing).

Interestingly, many philosophers believe the ego to be an *inhabitant*, as if were, of one's consciousness.

It becomes in transcending the ego that one is able to experience [1] increased rest and relaxation (from the questioning, analyzing, judging and scheming of the ego), [2] increased inner knowing (gnosis), [3] an enhanced sense of oneness with all creation, [4] increased creativity, stillness and clarity, and [5] a sense of liberation (from conflict and stress as well as from a sense of needing to defend the ego). [78]

The *Bhagavad-Gita* (the eternal message of spiritual wisdom from ancient India) talks about transcending the ego.

---

[78] *Transcending the Ego: Healing Egocentricity via Soul Connection* article accessed on April 20, 2011 at http://www.brothermichael.org.uk/resources/soul.htm

The word Gita means song and the word Bhagavad means God; often the Bhagavad-Gita is called the Song of God.

One can locate the Bhagavad-Gita in the historical epic Mahabharata (as written by Vedavyasa).

The Mahabharata, a significantly voluminous book, covers the history of the earth from the time of creation (in relation only to India).

Composed in 100,000 rhyming quatrain couplets, the Mahabharata is seven times the size of the Iliad (as written by Homer). It was written to also include all of the people in the world (who are outside of the Vedic culture). The Mahabharata, then, contains the essence of the Vedas.

It is said that in studying the Bhagavad-Gita, one will gain "accurate, fundamental knowledge about God, the ultimate truth, creation, birth and death, the results of actions, the eternal soul, liberation and the purpose, as well as the goal, of human existence." [79]

---

[79] http://www.bhagavad-gita.org/Articles/faq.html

Those that teach enlightenment (based on the information that stems from India, including the Bhagavad-Gita) all agree on one aspect: transcending the ego. If wanting to advance on a spiritual level, this must be accomplished.

The ego is crafty "to the point of deluding the person that is in the public eye; that they themselves have transcended the ego and others have not. It is *impossible to transcend the ego being in the public eye*. The ego will take advantage of any open door of opportunity for attention, which includes feeling special, being number one within a group, having people follow you, having control over others, and playing the victim." [80]

The ego exists in the form of emotions, feelings, beliefs and desires. To transcend the ego does not mean that we get rid of it; it simply means that you must learn to recognize it for what it is: an illusion (of separation) to which all are attached.

---

[80] *Transcending the Ego: Number One Priority* article accessed on April 20, 2011 at http://clearlyenlight.com/transcending-the-ego

In knowing, believing and accepting that you are no different from anyone else, because everything exists in the oneness of creation (which means that you fully acknowledge and recognize that you are something much greater than the egoic self), you are on your way to transcending the ego.

Free from both prejudice and judgment, you experience a deep sense of complete freedom.

You are not here to destroy the ego.

You are not here to dissolve the ego.

You are not here to kill the ego.

Instead, you are here to learn to become the detached observer. Likewise, you are also here to still the chatter in your mind. You are here to transcend the ego, which has a need to protect, defend and secure your physical identity (social status, reputation (which sometimes also translates as having power over other people), nationality, religion, closed belief systems), so that both mind and spirit (heart) can merge together, thereby working in unison.

We need to become "aware of our individual identities while simultaneously developing an expanded sense of global consciousness. Then we need to make sure both of these levels of awareness are aligned." [81]

The realization that you are more than just your ego (emotions, feelings, beliefs, desires, life experiences) is what allows you to begin to engage the world more fully, more completely, more consciously.

One successfully transforms (transcends) the ego by recognizing the fact that thoughts and behaviours at the individual (personal) level also impact thoughts and behaviours at the global (collective) level.

This is the very level from which one must begin this expansive work.

As you come to realize that you are part of the macrocosm (the bigger picture, the same stream of consciousness to which all are connected), you will have reconciled yourself

---

[81] *The War on Ego* article accessed on April 20, 2011 at
http://www.stevepavlina.com/blog/2008/03/the-war-on-ego/

with the knowingness that "if you can live constructively as an individual, and if you can influence enough of the other cells to make similar changes, you'll have a positive impact on shifting the larger body [of humanity] to more constructive behaviours." [82]

When I continue to align my choices with the higher good, knowing and believing that my choices are also serving to help others, I feel as if I am mysteriously guided and directed to the right circumstances, the right people, and the right situations. It must also be remembered that when you help another, you are also helping yourself. In short, achieving global consciousness, one individual at a time, is central to this philosophy.

The main caution, however, is that "you have to stay focused on the overlap between your individual good and the good of humanity. This takes a bit of practice because it's a different way of thinking about life than most people are taught. We're encouraged to think about how our

---

[82] *The War on Ego* article accessed on April 20, 2011 at
http://www.stevepavlina.com/blog/2008/03/the-war-on-ego/

actions affect the people closest to us, but not the entire body of humanity. There is an effect though, and it does make a difference." [83]

Transcendence resides within. The spirit that exists within is both formless and eternal. It becomes in acknowledging and living this knowledge that the ego loses its power. Seeking and claiming the power within is the only way to transcend. It was Isaac the Syrian who explained *the purpose of silence* as *awakening the mind to God*. [84]

Interestingly, there are many who claim that Stonehenge is a center for this spiritual transcendence. Given the proven acoustical properties, and knowing that sound equates to vibration, it is also a known fact that altered states of consciousness can be reached "through beat tones and rhythmic sessions at certain frequencies." [85]

---

[83] *The War on Ego* article accessed on April 20, 2011 at http://www.stevepavlina.com/blog/2008/03/the-war-on-ego/
[84] http://www.theosophical.org/publications/quest-magazine/1432
[85] *Stonehenge: A Spiritual Transformational Tool* article accessed on April 19, 2011 at http://aphroditeastrology.com/2009/12/stonehenge-spiritual-transcendence-tool.html

This is why "monks chant, those of Jewish faith rock back and forth (davening) while praying and indigenous people incorporate drumming into their rituals. This is also why Rave participants are easily induced into trance-like states. These rhythmic actions actually produce a clinically measurable effect on the brain." [86]

It is through rhythmic sessions and beat tones (binaural beats) that the brain reaches what is referred to as a state of coherence.

Coherence is reached when "waves in phase and of one wavelength simultaneously are generated in the different parts of the brain. This synchrony between the waves make the brain run like an optimal brain and a deep state of altered consciousness can be achieved. The frequencies that generate these altered states of consciousness on the human brain are known as Alpha and Theta waves." [87]

---

[86] *Stonehenge: A Spiritual Transformational Tool* article accessed on April 19, 2011 at http://aphroditeastrology.com/2009/12/stonehenge-spiritual-transcendence-tool.html

[87] Ibid.

Stonehenge researchers have noticed that "the side of the rocks facing the interior center of the circle were carved out somewhat to produce a concave dip in the face of the rock. This was done purposefully and for a reason. It appears that the acoustical qualities of Stonehenge are such that, when the proper rhythm is achieved through beat tones (drumming), Stonehenge actually begins to produce Alpha wave frequencies at 10 HZ," [88] frequencies that are "necessary to achieve altered states of consciousness that allow for astral planing or astral projection (out of body experiences)." [89]

In addition, the researchers were able to reproduce the acoustical affects of Stonehenge using binaural beat tones. They "played them for research subjects and then studied their brain wave patterns. Beat tones that were played with the Stonehenge acoustical properties produced near perfect

---

[88] *Stonehenge: A Spiritual Transformational Tool* article accessed on April 19, 2011 at http://aphroditeastrology.com/2009/12/stonehenge-spiritual-transcendence-tool.html
[89] Ibid.

brainwave patterns conducive to producing altered states of consciousness for the individual." [90]

Imagine, if you will, "an ancient ritual at Stonehenge. The entire circle is literally ringing loudly in Alpha wave frequencies, producing binaural beat tones in the brain and beat vibrations in the physical body that can be felt. Your brain is entering a state of altered consciousness while you are dancing in rhythm with the flickering flames of the burning fires." [91]

According to quantum physics, we are all made up of subatomic particles. Given that subatomic particles "can *bounce* in and out of different dimensions ... then this means that, technically, human beings can do the same." [92]

Theoretically speaking, does not this suggest that human beings possess the ability for inter-dimensional travel?

---

[90] *Stonehenge: A Spiritual Transformational Tool* article accessed on April 19, 2011 at http://aphroditeastrology.com/2009/12/stonehenge-spiritual-transcendence-tool.html
[91] Ibid.
[92] Ibid.

Knowing that Stonehenge appears to be "a perfectly composed mechanism for producing Alpha waves necessary to reach the altered state of consciousness for astral transcendence," [93] this begs the question that this webauthor also posits ... what may have happened to the people of Stonehenge?

Author David Darling refers to the pivotal moment in awakening as being the switchover from "normal dualistic mode of thinking to the selfless experience of transcendence." [94] Known by a multitude of different names (satori, nirvana, Tao, enlightenment, zoning, bliss), this fundamental mystical feeling, *The Perennial Philosophy*, may come "after years of asceticism, study, and devotion to some particular religious or meditation system." [95]

---

[93] *Stonehenge: A Spiritual Transformational Tool* article accessed on April 19, 2011 at http://aphroditeastrology.com/2009/12/stonehenge-spiritual-transcendence-tool.html
[94] http://www.daviddarling.info/works/ZenPhysics/ZenPhysics_ch13.html
[95] Ibid.

For most ordinary folk, it may arrive "out of the blue, unbidden and unsought" [96] given that "the very act of seeking may block or hinder the experience of enlightenment." [97]

The feeling of transcendent unity "is the same for everyone when it happens, since there is only one reality. However, problems ensue in translating this feeling into words. Even greater difficulties arise when others, who have not had the experience themselves, try to convey, second hand or third hand, what the fundamental teaching consisted of." [98]

From the reasonably clear and simple message of Gautama Buddha, "the vast and intricate system of religious philosophy that is Buddhism has sprung. Thousands of books and many millions of words have been set down on the subject, often in a style that only a lifetime devotee or learned academic could penetrate, but the irony is that

---

[96]

http://www.daviddarling.info/works/ZenPhysics/ZenPhysics_ch13.html
[97] Ibid.
[98] Ibid.

language and symbolism are anathema to the basic message of Buddha, which is all about *direct experience and unadulterated being.* And the same is true of Christianity. The central teaching of Jesus, a flesh-and-blood human being like you and me, was to *forget yourself and get in touch with the real world.*" [99]

Mind you, there can be "no proof of transcendence without the necessary self-transformation. Adopting an attitude of humility, and recognizing one's lack of knowledge, in order to seriously consider a transcendental philosophy, can be a beneficial exercise in and of itself." [100]

In the words of Albert Einstein ... *there are moments when one feels free from one's own identification with human limitations and inadequacies. At such moments, one imagines that one stands on some spot of a small planet, gazing in amazement at the cold, yet profoundly moving,*

---

[99]
http://www.daviddarling.info/works/ZenPhysics/ZenPhysics_ch13.html
[100] *Transition to Transcendence* article accessed on April 23, 2011 at http://www.cejournal.org/GRD/Wolff.htm

beauty of the eternal, the unfathomable: life and death flow into one, and there is neither evolution nor destiny; only being.

Clearly, this was an individual who understood his purpose, both as a scientist as well as a human being. Ultimately, what needs to be transcended are the limiting beliefs, the ignorance, the victim consciousness and the anger, all of which hold us back from our true selves.

Once your consciousness transcends "into quantum realms, you will not be above others or better than others, but you will be much more present in the here and now, channelling into space/time the grace of your higher consciousness." [101]

It was also Albert Einstein who said ... *The intuitive mind is a sacred gift and the rational mind is a faithful servant. We have created a society that honours the servant and has forgotten the gift.*

---

[101] *Becoming Galactic: Presuppositions of Quantum Consciousness* blog article accessed on April 23, 2011 at http://www.becoming-galactic.org/presupp8.html

There is no better time, than now, to both acknowledge and embrace this outstanding gift.

There are many different words – gnosis, satori, bodhi, nirvana, kensho and moksha – all of which describe aspects of enlightenment.

Believing something (perhaps because many others believe the same thing and it is more reassuring to be able to continue to do so) *is not the same as knowing* (and having experienced) something (for yourself), for therein lies your wisdom, your truth.

To awaken to the preponderance of oneness, to awaken to the integrity of harmony, to awaken to the completeness of unity, these are our ultimate reasons for being. Such is the very evolution of all humankind.

As I have stated before, when one is adamant that this is the way things are (end of story, there is no more), one has become closed to that which is new, to that which is evolving, to that which may be a most plausible possibility.

How, then, can one be open to gnosis?

How, then, can one be open to transcending previously held beliefs?

How, then, can one begin to experience their truest nature for themselves?

The most important concept in Gnostic philosophy is that which is called polarity.

In this instance, polarity can be described as *the presence or manifestation of two opposite or contrasting principles or tendencies*.

Polarity, then, is simply a duality of opposites that are essentially one, as in good/evil, night/day, yes/no, masculine/feminine, black/white, life/death, much akin to the heads or tails of any given coin.

In short, you cannot have one without the other.

Philosophies that "adopt an either/or approach teach that we are *either* separate *or* all one."[102] Hmmmm; either completely separate or one, without any other possibility in between. Having seen through the illusion of separation, I think that I will pass on this outmoded definition of my existence.

By comparison, however, Gnostic philosophy is "based on an understanding of polarity, so it adopts a both/and approach, teaching that we are *both* one *and* many,"[103] which simply equates to everyone being the same energy as the one stream of universal consciousness that exists, while also experiencing themselves as individuated aspects of the same.

As spiritual beings, if we acknowledge that God/dess is also this same stream of consciousness, from whence we have come, then, so, too, are we God/dess (albeit, for the most part, *un*actualized).

---

[102] Freke, Timothy, and Gandy, Peter. *The Gospel of the Second Coming* (page 84). Carlsbad, CA: Hay House, Inc.
[103] Ibid.

Taking it one step further, if we are all God/dess, then there is only one God/dess experiencing existence through the many individual stories that continue to be written.

Now *that* is a most enlightening reckoning, is it not?

Gnosis is a "direct realization of your essential nature that manifests as a tangible experience in the body," [104] one that you will be able to identify through love. The Beatles were so right when they wrote that *love is all we need* because it is love that we feel when "we see through separateness and recognize our essential oneness." [105]

It is this form of unconditional love that allows us to feel both the happiness of another as well as their pain.

It is this form of unconditional love that allows us to realize that when one suffers, so, too, do we all suffer.

If hurting another translates to hurting yourself, why, then, do we continue to operate in such a manner?

---

[104] Freke, Timothy, and Gandy, Peter. *The Gospel of the Second Coming* (page 90). Carlsbad, CA: Hay House, Inc.
[105] Ibid, page 91.

It is this form of unconditional love, when experienced in its truest, transcendent, sense, that opens our hearts to love (and forgive) everyone and everything, further allowing us to embrace things as they are, without judgment. This is what I refer to as compassionate allowing.

Spiritual awakening begins "when we start to doubt our conditioning and explore our own insights," [106] thereby becoming independent freethinkers by following our hearts. "We need to individuate as a separate some-one before we can become conscious of the All-One." [107] Once again, therein lies the paradox, the polarity, the duality of our very selves.

We are here to wake up to the illusion (separation) and thoroughly love life, to simply love BEing, because in so doing, we will have progressed from the beginning of ego development to the final stages of spiritual enlightenment; in essence, two parts of the same process.

---

[106] Freke, Timothy, and Gandy, Peter. *The Gospel of the Second Coming* (page 133). Carlsbad, CA: Hay House, Inc.
[107] Ibid.

Timothy Freke and Peter Gandy sum everything up so marvelously well when they write that gnosis "is the recognition of our essential oneness *through* the story of separateness." [108]

When you are one with the present moment, with the now, you are experiencing gnosis.

When you are loving the present moment, you are also experiencing gnosis.

When your life is all about creating Heaven here on Earth in your day to day life, so, too, are you experiencing gnosis.

It is this very moment that is "the mystical marriage of opposites. Right now you are the Author and the story. The mystery and the manifest. Possibility and actuality. You are the pre-conceptual presence of the Primal Imagination expressing itself as everything that is." [109]

---

[108] Freke, Timothy, and Gandy, Peter. *The Gospel of the Second Coming* (page 170). Carlsbad, CA: Hay House, Inc.
[109] Ibid, page 191.

Now is the time to become conscious of BEing (one and all), to simply love BEing, so that you will be in love with BEing.

Who would have thought that it was this simple?

Oneness can mean [1] *unity of thought, feeling, belief* as well as [2] *a strong feeling of closeness or affinity* (as in a union with something or someone).

Oneness can also refer to the concept that One is all and all is One, with each individual, of course, being a microcosm of the macrocosm.

This process of union, also referred to as Henosis, culminates in deification, meaning that each man, in replacing the concept of God as creator with themselves as creators, builders, craftsmen of their own lives (with their own life being their greatest work), in merging with the Monad, in turn, becomes God. [110]

Just as it is most difficult to describe Oneness adequately in words (primarily because it needs to be experienced), so, too, is it the same with Zen.

---

[110] http://en.wikipedia.org/wiki/Henosis

If one were to describe Zen, one might say that Zen is a "practice that helps man to penetrate to his true self through cross-legged sitting (Zazen) and to vitalize this self in daily life." [111]

Zen involves daily Zazen practice (as developed in ancient India). The word Zen comes from *dhyana* (meaning to think) which "appears in the pre-Buddhist <u>Upanishads</u>. This was the form of Zazen used by the Buddha, although his philosophic standpoint differed." [112]

In Zazen, the important point "is to harmonize body, breathing, and mind. The half or full paryanka posture is used. Exhaling and inhaling settle to a calm rhythm. Breathing plays a vital role; in India it is called prana, or life. To harmonize the mind is to dissolve the perplexities and delusions that disturb our minds." [113]

---

[111] *Zen in Daily Life* article accessed on April 23, 2011 at
http://www.zenki.com/index.php?lang=en&page=Masunaga01
[112] Ibid.
[113] Ibid.

While nothing is sought in Zazen, the results are said to be substantial.

Repeated practice seems to invigorate the involuntary nervous system, thereby strengthening the Solar Plexus.

Some Japanese psychologists have credited Zazen with "facilitating recovery from some illnesses, strengthening spiritual resources and lessening neuroticism, changing mental attitudes to eliminate bad habits, restraining destructive impulses, developing greater insight into situations, and fostering freedom from anxiety." [114]

In addition, results of recent scientific experiments seem to indicate that Zazen also reduces the modulation of brain waves, meaning that Zazen "prepares the body and mind for the next stage of vital activity." [115]

In Zazen, the only reality that exists is the here and now.

---

[114] *Zen in Daily Life* article accessed on April 23, 2011 at
http://www.zenki.com/index.php?lang=en&page=Masunaga01
[115] Ibid.

While feelings and emotions "exist as part of the physical experience, by not clinging to them we are able to experience freedom." [116]

Each act, therefore, becomes one that leads to self-mastery (meaning composure and tranquility of mind).

Zazen, therefore, is "both something one does (as in sitting cross-legged, with proper posture and correct breathing) as well as something one essentially is (meaning one comes to the profound realization of their original nature, as well as the realization itself)." [117]

It becomes with time and sincere effort in Zazen practice, that mind and body (self and universe) are experienced as one. This condition of effortless concentration is known as *Samadhi* (a form of enlightenment).

---

[116] *Zen in Daily Life* article accessed on April 23, 2011 at
http://www.zenki.com/index.php?lang=en&page=Masunaga01
[117] Ibid.

The "second and more difficult aim is the actualization of the *Bodhisattva* (Enlightened Being) ideal, whereby love and compassion for all beings is developed."[118]

As one's practice of Zazen ripens, "one becomes more alive, more creative; filled with the longing to actualize the Bodhisattva spirit in every moment and every aspect of daily life."[119]

In summation, Zen emphasizes experiential wisdom in the attainment of enlightenment. As such, it de-emphasizes theoretical knowledge (in favor of direct self-realization through meditation and dharma practice).

Anne Thomas has been blogging from Sendai since the horrific March 11, 2011 earthquake that devastated Japan, triggering a huge tsunami that slammed into the north eastern coast of the country.

---

[118] *What is Zen: A Brief Explanation* article accessed on April 23, 2011 at http://www.amacord.com/taste/essays/zen.html
[119] Ibid.

In her April 2, 2011 entry, she speaks about the sense of oneness that currently exists in Sendai. [120] A truly magnificent piece, I encourage all readers to further explore these postings from the heart.

In the words of Albert Einstein ... *A human being is a part of a whole, called by us the universe, a part limited in time and space. He experiences himself, his thoughts and feelings, as something separated from the rest ... a kind of optical delusion of his consciousness. This delusion is a kind of prison for us, restricting us to our personal desires and to affection for a few persons nearest to us. Our task must be to free ourselves from this* prison *by widening our circles of compassion to embrace all living creatures and the whole of nature in its beauty.*

Thereafter, we shall begin to fully understand and embrace the reality of oneness.

---

[120] Thomas, Anne. (April 2, 2011) *A sense of oneness in Sendai* blog posting accessed on April 23, 2011 at http://www.odemagazine.com/blogs/readers_blog/25239/a_sense_of_o neness_in_sendai

Connection, caring, cooperation and compassion; these are what constitute harmony.

The Indigenous peoples have long lived in balanced harmony with the totality of creation, taking only what was needed. This is a principle of great importance that we must learn to embrace once again.

Living in harmony with nature (while protecting both the environment as well as other living beings that inhabit the planet), requires that we become stewards (guardians) of Mother Earth.

She, too, is a living organism, that needs to be nurtured and cared for in a loving manner.

Living in balanced harmony with nature, and each other, allows one to rediscover the ancient wisdom of love, inner peace and happiness.

Harmony is both an ancient social ideal as well as an actual life choice.

How, then, does one, work to promote harmony?

The foremost necessity becomes *being able to forgive and forget the past*; one must always be prepared to start anew.

Unless you actually "see something for your own selves, or hear it with your own ears, do not believe it. If somebody tells you something unbecoming, know that a man has different moods; we are not perfect. If we have love for others, that very love beautifies even the worst of things. You have to see from that level. That is the only way." [121]

In taking the word world (w-o-r-l-d) and eliminating the letter L from the word, "what remains is Word. The Word is God. If you eliminate yourself (the ego), the thought that

---

[121]   *Harmony* excerpt from a talk with Sant Kirpal Singh in Washington, DC, on September 2, 1963 accessed on April 23, 2011 at http://www.kirpalsingh-teachings.org/index.php/en/talks/431-harmony.html

you are doing it, you are God's. You become the mouthpiece of God." [122]

These are most profound words, are they not?

In remaining true to your divine selves, in appreciating those around you (for whatever it is that they are able to do), in working for the sake of the common cause (as in the greater good), in living your best each day, know that God/dess is continuing to work through you.

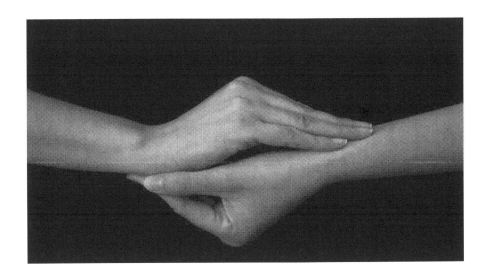

---

[122]   *Harmony* excerpt from a talk with Sant Kirpal Singh in Washington, DC, on September 2, 1963 accessed on April 23, 2011 at http://www.kirpalsingh-teachings.org/index.php/en/talks/431-harmony.html

Every biological system appears to thrive as a result of cooperation. Why, then, are we, as an organism, so hell-bent on competition as opposed to cooperation?

We are all connected from an electrical (energy) perspective (because everything is energy), a vibrational perspective (because everything sends out vibrational energies) and a substance perspective (because the entirety of our continually expanding universe is made of the same atoms, molecules, electrons and subatomic particles).

In short, we are connected to everything that exists (known as well as unknown). Even more intimately, "God is in you and all around you ... involved in every thought you think and every action you take." [123]

Believing in the theory of separateness is what continues to bring "needless arguments and conflicts, violence, wars,

---

[123] *I Am Connected To All* article accessed on April 23, 2011 at http://www.unhinderedliving.com/connectedtoall.html

being overly suspicious of other people, and other negative and ultimately destructive events and behaviors. Believing in the theory of connectedness brings us: fruitful discussions with others, an avoidance of violence and wars, believing in the goodness of oneself and others, creating and keeping good friendships and relationships, and ultimately creating a better world for oneself and for others." [124]

While you can still be your own person, with your own interests, desires, and goals, you are also able to "realize that you are, in some way, connected to everyone else on this planet. This way, you can have your own life, and also ensure that others have their own lives, but also contribute to a safer, more peaceful, more accepting, and more positive world." [125]

It is love, often appearing so distant and obscure at times, that continues to remain the cure.

---

[124] *Super State: Why We Are All Connected To Each Other* article accessed on April 23, 2011 at http://blog.super-state.com/2008/06/20/why-we-are-all-connected-to-each-other.aspx
[125] Ibid.

Tom Shadyac is known for having directed such movie hits as Ace Ventura: Pet Detective, The Nutty Professor, Liar Liar, Patch Adams, Dragonfly, Bruce Almighty and Evan Almighty. His most current documentary is entitled I AM. In the course of exploring his own personal journey, which includes both *the nature of humanity* [126] as well as the *world's ever growing addiction to materialism,* [127] Shadyac interviews scientists, psychologists, artists, authors, philosophers, religious leaders, environmentalists and entrepreneurs. [128]

The documentary asks two central questions; namely,

---

[126] Oldenburg, Ann. (March 24, 2011) *Director Tom Shadyac: "I've been called crazy many times"* article featured in USA Today and accessed on April 20, 2011 at http://content.usatoday.com/communities/entertainment/post/2011/03/director-tom-shadyac-ive-been-called-crazy-many-times/1?csp=34

[127] Harris, Paul. (January 16, 2011) *Tom Shadyac: the hot movie director who turned a camera on the Hollywood world he gave up* article featured in The Observer and accessed on April 20, 2011 at http://www.guardian.co.uk/film/2011/jan/16/tom-shadyac-hollywood-movies-film

[128] http://iamthedoc.com/thefilm

[1] What is wrong with the world?

[2] What can we do about it?

Only *you* can answer these most deliberate and piercing questions for yourself.

In addition, however, I would also add the following questions for contemplation.

[1] What is it that truly sustains you?

[2] What is it that fills your heart?

[3] What is it that helps you become the best person you can be?

[4] What is it that strengthens your heart, enabling you to be of service, while offering compassion, to others?

Ironically, in the process of trying to figure out what was *wrong* with the world, Shadyac discovered that there was actually "more *right* than he ever imagined. He learned that the heart, not the brain, may be man's primary organ of intelligence, and that human consciousness and emotions can actually affect the physical world." [129]

In keeping with his own life story, Shadyac demonstrates that "money is not a pathway to happiness. In fact, he even learns that in some native cultures, gross materialism is equated with insanity." [130]

Shadyac also discovered that "contrary to conventional thinking, cooperation, and not competition, may be nature's most fundamental operating principle. Thus, I AM shows *consensus decision-making is the norm* amongst many species, from insects and birds to deer and primates." [131] Most assuredly, we still have much to learn.

The film further discovers that "humans actually function better and remain healthier when expressing positive emotions, such as love, care, compassion, and gratitude, versus their negative counterparts: anxiety, frustration, anger

---

[129] http://iamthedoc.com/thefilm
[130] Ibid.
[131] Ibid.

and fear," [132] a connection that I, too, have continued to highlight in my books.

It was a revelation to Shadyac that "for tens of thousands of years, Indigenous cultures taught a very different story about our inherent goodness. Now, following this ancient wisdom, science is discovering a plethora of evidence about our hardwiring for connection and compassion, from the Vagus Nerve, which releases oxytocin at simply witnessing a compassionate act, to the Mirror Neuron, which causes us to literally feel another person's pain." [133]

In fact, it was Darwin himself, who, while "misunderstood to believe exclusively in our competitiveness, actually noted that humankind's real power comes in their ability to perform complex tasks together, to sympathize and cooperate." [134]

---

[132] http://iamthedoc.com/thefilm
[133] Ibid.
[134] Ibid.

It is with great wit, warmth, curiosity, and masterful storytelling skills, that Shadyac reveals what science now tells us is one of the principal truths of the universe, a message that is as simple as it is significant: *we are all connected to each other and to everything around us.* [135]

For some of us, this is the transformative piece.

---

[135] http://iamthedoc.com/thefilm

Enlightenment

The following words, well worth sharing and reflecting upon, are not my own. They belong to Osho, a professor of philosophy, who travelled throughout India in the 1960's as a public speaker.

Meditation will not give you enlightenment, remember. No technique can ever give you enlightenment; enlightenment is not technical. Meditation can only prepare the ground. Meditation can only open the door.

Enlightenment is not something like an achievement; one cannot achieve it. One has to disappear for it to happen. It is a happening and it happens only in the absence of the ego.

The ego is a doer, and enlightenment happens in a state of nondoing; it is simply the realization of who you are; it is not a question of achievement.

Enlightenment simply means being in a state of let-go. Enlightenment simply means undoing what the society has done to you.

What your parents have imposed upon you, throw it away; what the society has conditioned you to be, put it aside. Reassert your being.

Love yourself and respect yourself, and try to be just yourself.

Enlightenment is possible, but it will be possible only when you are ready to lose yourself. That is the meaning of Jesus' saying when he says, "If you lose, you will gain. If you don't lose, you will lose."

In losing is the gain. In forgetting is the remembrance. In dissolving, you become crystallized.

In a single moment, in one stroke, you can become enlightened. It is not a gradual process, because enlightenment is not something that you have to invent. It is something that you have to discover. It is already there.

It is not something that you have to manufacture. Close your eyes and see it there. Be silent and have a taste of it. Your very nature is what I call enlightenment. It is you, your very core.

The idea of enlightenment is to remain in the present moment – not to go into the past, which is no more, not to go into the future, which is not yet — because if you go into past and future, you are going to miss the present moment, which is the only reality. Just be here, now.

And if you are here and now, enlightenment comes of its own accord. It is not a goal that you have to reach. It is not somewhere far away, so that you have to travel a path to it. It comes to you, you never go to it. It is not your doing, it is a happening.

My religion is nothing but the art of living, the art of loving. And if you can manage two things, total life and total love, the third thing, enlightenment, will come of its own accord. You have earned it.

You need not seek it, you deserve it. It is a reward from existence to those people who have respected life, loved, lived, danced, enjoyed.

Reprinted from

http://www.oshoquotes.net/2009/12/osho-quotes-on-enlightenment/

Conclusion

In all of the research that I have undertaken, over the course of the past twenty years, it is clear that humanity is here to awaken to several foremost, and necessary, agenda items, so to speak.

[1] To remember *who you really are*.

As sparks of the Divine, we are life (light) itself. Source energy, with whom we are one, is limitless, meaning that so, too, are we limitless.

[2] To remember *why you are here*.

We are here to recognize our invisible connection to All That Is. We are here to identify that the Creator lives within us; that, together, we are co-creators.

The universal creative mind, meaning your mind as well as that of the rest of the universe, is powered by intelligence. The physical world, therefore, is made up of both energy as well as ideas (projected thoughts).

[3] To recognize that *separation is an illusion*; that we have always been connected to the Infinite Source.

[4] To understand that *both polarity, as well as negativity, are catalysts.*

As tools, each provides us with a free will opportunity to move towards becoming actualized as authentic selves. A soul can only choose positivity in a world where the polar opposite also abounds. That having been said, does not the Creator reside in all things? It is the illusion that shows you who you are not.

[5] To understand that *you have the power to express your reality* (within the game) as you wish (through your thoughts, words, actions and deeds) and that *the world becomes your mirror*, casting back at you the reflection of who you are at any given moment in time.

Everything begins with a thought; hence, you must be careful what you think about, you must be careful what you express, you must be careful what you act upon.

You get what you expect to receive, meaning that your dominant thoughts (because of your constant attention) are what shall manifest in your reality.

If you want a new reality, you must think new thoughts and create new beliefs.

What you think about is directly related to what you will see in your life (in the form of relationships, circumstances and events), for therein lies the crucial difference between conscious creation (when you are creating with intent) and unconscious creation (when you are creating by default).

As negative thoughts arise, take the time to catch yourself, sending out a more positive response. This is the very transformative process that you are here to engage in.

There is no such thing as coincidence. Nothing happens by chance. As per quantum physics, you are the creator of your world, of your reality (within the game).

Everything is made up of subatomic particles (energy). This energy exists as waves spread out over time and space.

It is through your observation, your attention, as well as your intention (to create something), that these energy waves are transformed into physical particles, appearing duly solid to the observer.

Nothing exists unless we are observing it, meaning that *we can*, quite literally, *think something into existence.*

[6] To *listen to your inner voice.*

It is essential that you learn to trust your inner guidance. You do this by following your heart.

[7] To *find your own truth.*

Do not take the truth of another, myself included, to be the final and ultimate truth. It is imperative that you learn to make use of discernment when attempting to identify that which resonates with you.

Only you can ascertain that which feels true to you.

Take the time to sit quietly in meditation, asking the Creator to guide your path.

Should negative feelings arise, they are to be seen as mere tools that can assist you in becoming an authentic human being.

[8] To remember that *you are an evolving soul*, doing your utmost to master yourself each day.

You are here to develop your mind (working on your thoughts and feelings).

You are here to develop your soul (in the cultivating of both compassion as well as compassionate allowing).

You are here to understand that as you change, from day to day, so, too, do your truths (and energy) change.

[9] To *celebrate life*.

You are here to celebrate, with gratitude, all that you continue to create for yourself.

The life experiences, as created by you, allow and enable you to work on yourself; to grow, to develop, to transform.

Take the time to experience those things that instill you with a sense of deep passion, inner contentment and sheer jubilation.

This is what allows you to go with your creative flow.

As a writer, I feel that being in the creative flow is most reminiscent of the following words attributed to Andrew Cohen, editor of EnlightenNext Magazine.

Think about your experience of those moments when you are most creatively engaged. What does it feel like? Being in a creative "flow" can be ecstatic and, simultaneously, there is an often surprising sense of urgency to bring into being that which you can sense is possible. That's why great artists or scientists will work day and night, neglecting to eat or sleep. They are driven by a vision, something just beyond their reach that will not let them rest until they have brought it into reality. That drive is the very same impetus that caused the whole universe to burst forth, fourteen billion years ago, and is now expressing itself through the body, mind, heart, and talents of an inspired human being.

When you feel that creative flow, often you discover a part of yourself you are not normally aware of but which feels more like your "self" than the person you usually think you are. It's like plugging in to a deeper source of energy and passion that transcends whatever limitations you ordinarily assume. A deeper, more authentic part of your self is creatively released. That's why such moments are so fulfilling; it's not just the creative work you produce, but the experience of being more alive, more connected, more in touch with a sense of meaning and purpose.

This is exactly how I feel when I am researching and writing. I know that I am plugged into a higher source, if you will, whilst following the dictates of my heart.

When you, too, have found your creative flow, you will most assuredly know.

Existing within feelings of lightness and joy, peacefulness and exuberance, this, too, is key to your own personal awakening.

In a posting, courtesy of Steve Beckow's site, [136] David Wilcock writes about how disaster can be averted by one's state of consciousness.

Wilcock shares that the reality is that "the world is offering us precisely what we need to be awakened — on a mass, worldwide level," [137] meaning that "the greater objective is to understand the process, and understand that you, right now, reading this, have far more control over the outcome than you may have ever realized." [138]

How can this be so, you ask?

According to Wilcock, "the real battle that is being fought is for how you think and feel each day. Once you understand this, you can become an active participant in the solution. It doesn't require you to subscribe to anything, pay any money or even leave the house. All it requires is a positive attitude:

---

[136] http://stevebeckow.com/
[137] http://stevebeckow.com/2011/05/david-wilcock-disaster-can-be-averted-by-our-state-of-consciousness/
[138] Ibid.

to have love be the primary force that runs through your thoughts, emotions and actions." [139]

The real challenge that we are being offered is "to see love where others can only see hate." [140] While you can hate all you want, should that be your choice, "you are voting for disasters to occur if you stay in this state of consciousness. This is final exam time. It is critical that each of us move into a state of loving kindness, as best we are able in our own humble ways, in order to ensure the safety and security of this planet." [141]

In keeping with the proven, geometric, circuitry flow patterns, "when we are in a state of loving kindness and peace, we get smooth brainwaves. These brainwaves in turn strengthen the spin field in gravity and the Earth is made healthy," [142] meaning that our brainwaves merge with the flow.

---

[139] http://stevebeckow.com/2011/05/david-wilcock-disaster-can-be-averted-by-our-state-of-consciousness/
[140] Ibid.
[141] Ibid.
[142] Ibid.

By comparison, "when we are in a state of static and chaos, our brainwaves get very choppy and violent. This literally affects the spin of gravity and creates stress in the Earth." [143]

Simply put, this means that "when enough people create static and chaos, the spin fields cannot flow in a given area the way they should. This creates a pressure build-up in the surrounding area, because the current needs to go somewhere. Earthquakes, volcanoes and natural disasters are the result." [144]

Truly, we have more of an effect on the Earth's immune system than most have ever postulated to be true. We must take the time to pull together and support each other, so that "the quality of our conscious interaction with each other again improves." [145]

This is what shall restore health to the planet.

---

[143] http://stevebeckow.com/2011/05/david-wilcock-disaster-can-be-averted-by-our-state-of-consciousness/
[144] Ibid.
[145] Ibid.

Should one wish to subscribe to Steve's site, click on Email Updates [146] towards the top right hand segment of the webpage. Thereafter, it is possible to view all archived mailings [147] as sent out by this fellow Canadian.

To sum everything up, Andrew Cohen also shares that *spiritual self-confidence fills one's heart with a love that is not dependent on external circumstances for its fullness. It's a love that is unshakable, unmoving, and indestructible. Such love, a love that transcends yet simultaneously embraces the world, is what compels human beings to evolve, from their own deepest depths, and to become better citizens of our world and our cosmos. Knowing the mysterious source of that love is knowing, before thought, that life is good. That inherent goodness is who we really are.*

It is my wish that a great many will resonate with the messages contained within this particular tome.

Namaste.

---

[146] http://stevebeckow.com/
[147] http://archive.feedblitz.com/715643

Braden, Gregg. (1995) *Awakening to Zero Point: The Collective Initiation.*

Braden, Gregg. (1997) *Walking Between the Worlds: The Science of Compassion.*

Braden, Gregg. (2000) *The Isaiah Effect: Decoding the Lost Science of Prayer and Prophecy.*

Braden, Gregg. (2000) *Beyond Zero Point: The Journey to Compassion.*

Braden, Gregg. (2004) *The God Code: The Secret of Our Past, The Promise of Our Future.*

Braden, Gregg. (2004) *The Divine Name: Sounds of the God Code.* (Audio Book)

Braden, Gregg. (2005) *The Lost Mode of Prayer.* (Audio CD)

Braden, Gregg. (2005) *Unleashing The Power of The God Code: The Mystery and Meaning of the Message in Our Cells*. (Audio CD)

Braden, Gregg. (2005) *An Ancient Magical Prayer: Insights from the Dead Sea Scrolls*. (Audio Book)

Braden, Gregg. (2005) *Speaking the Lost Language of God: Awakening the Forgotten Wisdom of Prayer, Prophecy and the Dead Sea Scrolls*. (Audio Book)

Braden, Gregg. (2005) *Awakening the Power of A Modern God: Unlock the Mystery and Healing of Your Spiritual DNA*. (Audio Book)

Braden, Gregg. (2006) *Secrets of The Lost Mode of Prayer*.

Braden, Gregg. (2007) *The Divine Matrix: Bridging Time, Space, Miracles and Belief*.

Bunick, Nick. (2010) *Time for Truth: A New Beginning*.

Chopra, Deepak. (1998) *The Path to Love: Spiritual Strategies for Healing*.

Chopra, Deepak. (2005) *Peace Is The Way: Bringing War and Violence to An End.*

Clark, Robert A. *The Christ Mind.* [148]

Coelho, Paulo. (1998) *The Alchemist.*

Coelho, Paulo. (2003) *Warrior Of The Light.*

Das, Lama Surys. (1998) *Awakening the Buddha Within.*

Das, Lama Surys. (2000) *Awakening to the Sacred: Creating a Spiritual Life From Scratch.*

Das, Lama Surys. (2001) *Awakening the Buddhist Heart: Integrating Love, Meaning and Connection into Every Part of Your Life.*

Das, Lama Surys. (2003) *Living Kindness: The Buddha's Ten Guiding Principles for a Blessed Life.*

---

[148] http://www.thechristmind.org/thechristmind.pdf

Das, Lama Surys. (2003) *Letting Go of the Person You Used To Be: Lessons on Change, Loss and Spiritual Transformation.*

Doucette, Michele. (2010) *A Travel in Time to Grand Pré.* (second edition)

Doucette, Michele. (2010) *The Ultimate Enlightenment For 2012: All We Need Is Ourselves.*

Doucette, Michele. (2010) *Turn Off The TV: Turn On Your Mind.*

Doucette, Michele. (2010) *Veracity At Its Best.*

Doucette, Michele. (2011) *Sleepers Awaken: The Time Is Now To Consciously Create Your Own Reality.*

Doucette, Michele. (2011) *Healing the Planet and Ourselves: How To Raise Your Vibration.*

Doucette, Michele. (2011) *You Are Everything: Everything Is You.*

Ford. (2005) *Becoming God.*

Ford, Debbie. (2010) *The 21 Day Consciousness Cleanse: A Breakthrough Program for Connecting with Your Soul's Deepest Purpose.*

Freke, Timothy. (2005) *Lucid Living.*

Freke, Timothy. (2009) *How Long Is Now? A Journey to Enlightenment and Beyond.*

Freke, Timothy, and Gandy, Peter. (2001) *The Jesus Mysteries: Was the Original Jesus a Pagan God?*

Freke, Timothy, and Gandy, Peter. (2002) *Jesus and The Lost Goddess: The Secret Teachings of the Original Christians.*

Freke, Timothy, and Gandy, Peter. (2006) *The Laughing Jesus: Religious Lies and Gnostic Wisdom.*

Freke, Timothy, and Gandy, Peter. (2007) *The Gospel of the Second Coming.*

Gawain, Shakti. (1993) *Living In The Light: A Guide to Personal and Planetary Transformation.*

Gawain, Shakti. (1999) *The Four Levels of Healing.*

Gawain, Shakti. (2000) *The Path of Transformation: How Healing Ourselves Can Change The World.*

Gawain, Shakti. (2003) *Reflections in The Light: Daily Thoughts and Affirmations.*

Goswami, Amit. (1995) *The Self-Aware Universe.*

Grof, Stanislav and Bennett, Hal Zina. (1993) *The Holotropic Mind: The Three Levels of Human Consciousness and How They Shape Our Lives.*

Hansard, Christopher. (2003) *The Tibetan Art of Positive Thinking.*

Hicks, Esther and Hicks, Jerry. (2004) *Ask and It Is Given: Learning to Manifest Your Desires.*

Hicks, Esther and Hicks, Jerry. (2004) *The Teachings of Abraham: Well-Being Cards.*

Hicks, Esther and Hicks, Jerry. (2005) *The Amazing Power of Deliberate Intent: Living the Art of Allowing.*

Hicks, Esther and Hicks, Jerry. (2006) *The Law of Attraction: The Basics of the Teachings of Abraham.*

Hicks, Esther and Hicks, Jerry. (2008) *The Astonishing Power of Emotions: Let Your Feelings Be Your Guide.*

Hicks, Esther and Hicks, Jerry. (2009) *The Vortex: Where The Law of Attraction Assembles all Cooperative Relationships.*

James, John. (2007) *The Great Field: Soul At Play In The Conscious Universe.*

Judd, Isha. (2008) *Why Walk When You Can Fly: Soar Beyond Your Fears and Love Yourself and Others Unconditionally.*

Koven, Jean-Claude. (2004) *Going Deeper: How To Make Sense of Your Life When Your Life Makes No Sense.*

Kribbe, Pamela. (2008) *The Jeshua Channelings: Christ Consciousness in a New Era.*

Lama, Dalai. (2004) *The Wisdom of Forgiveness: Intimate Conversations and Journey.*

McTaggart, Lynne. (2003) *The Field: The Quest For The Secret Force Of The Universe*.

McTaggart, Lynne. (2008) *The Intention Experiment: Using Your Thoughts to Change Your Life and the World*.

McTaggart, Lynne. (2011) *The Bond: Connecting Through the Space Between Us*.

Millman, Dan. (2000) *Way of the Peaceful Warrior*.

Millman, Dan. (1991) *Sacred Journey of the Peaceful Warrior*.

Millman, Dan. (1992) *No ordinary Moments: A Peaceful Warrior's Guide to Daily Life*.

Millman, Dan. (1995) *The Life You Were Born To Live*.

Millman, Dan. (1999) *Everyday Enlightenment*.

Moses, Jeffrey. (2002) *Oneness: Great Principles Shared By All Religions*.

Nichols, L. Joseph. (2000) *The Soul As Healer: Lessons in Affirmation, Visualization and Inner Power*.

Radin, Dean I. (2006) *Entangled Minds: Extrasensory Experiences in a Quantum Reality*.

Radin, Dean I. (2009) *The Conscious Universe: The Scientific Truth of Psychic Phenomena*.

Rennison, Susan Joy. (2008) *Tuning the Diamonds: Electromagnetism and Spiritual Evolution*.

Ruiz, Don Miguel. (1997) *The Four Agreements: A Practical Guide to Personal Freedom*.

Ruiz, Don Miguel. (1999) *The Mastery of Love: A Practical Guide to The Art of Relationship*.

Ruiz, Don Miguel. (2000) *The Four Agreements Companion Book*.

Ruiz, Don Miguel. (2004) *The Voice of Knowledge: A Practical Guide to Inner Peace*.

Ruiz, Don Miguel. (2009) *Fifth Agreement: A Practical Guide to Self-Mastery*.

Talbot, Michael. (1992) *The Holographic Universe*.

Talbot, Michael. (1993) *Mysticism and the New Physics*.

Tolle, Eckhart. (1999) *The Power of Now: A Guide to Spiritual Enlightenment*.

Tolle, Eckhart. (2001) *Practicing the Power of Now: Meditations, Exercises and Core Teachings for Living the Liberated Life*.

Tolle, Eckhart. (2001) *The Realization of Being: A Guide to Experiencing Your True Identity*. (Audio CD)

Tolle, Eckhart. (2003) *Stillness Speaks*.

Tolle, Eckhart. (2003) *Entering The Now*. (Audio CD)

Tolle, Eckhart. (2008) *A New Earth: Awakening to Your Life's Purpose*.

Twyman, James. (1998) *Emissary of Peace: A Vision of Light*.

Twyman, James. (2000) *The Secret of the Beloved Disciple*.

Twyman, James. (2000) *Portrait of the Master*.

Twyman, James. (2000) *Praying Peace: In Conversation with Gregg Braden and Doreen Virtue.*

Twyman, James. (2003) *The Proposing Tree.*

Twyman, James. (2008) *The Moses Code: The Most Powerful Manifestation Tool in the History of the World.*

Twyman, James. (2009) *The Kabbalah Code: A True Adventure.*

Twyman, James. (2009) *The Proof: A 40-Day Program for Embodying Oneness.*

Wolf, Fred Alan. (1989). *Taking the Quantum Leap: The New Physics for Nonscientists.*

Wolf, Fred Alan. (2000). *Mind Into Matter: A New Alchemy of Science and Spirit.*

Wolf, Fred Alan. (2002). *Matter Into Feeling: A New Alchemy of Science and Spirit.*

Wolf, Fred Alan. (2004). *The Yoga of Time Travel: How the Mind Can Defeat Time.*

Wolf, Myke. (2010). *Create from Being: Guide to Conscious Creation.*

Zukav, Gary. (1998) *The Seat of The Soul.*

Zukav, Gary. (2001) *Thoughts from The Seat of The Soul: Meditations for Souls in Process.*

Zukav, Gary and Francis, Linda. (2001) *The Heart of The Soul: Emotional Awareness.*

Zukav, Gary and Francis, Linda. (2003) *The Mind of The Soul: Responsible Choice.*

Zukav, Gary and Francis, Linda. (2003) *Self-Empowerment Journal: A Companion to The Mind of The Soul: Responsible Choice.*

Zukav, Gary. (2010) *Spiritual Partnership: The Journey to Authentic Power.*

Weisenthal, Simon. (1998) *The Sunflower: On the Possibilities and Limits of Forgiveness*

Website Bibliography

A New Earth: Are You Ready to be Awakened? [149]

A New Earth: Your Personal Workbook [150]

A New Earth: Exercises for Your Awakening [151]

Are Enlightenment and Transcendence Altered States (video by Charles T. Tart) [152]

Are Enlightenment and Transcendence Altered States (video by Jaron Lanier) [153]

---

[149] http://www.oprah.com/oprahsbookclub/A-New-Earth-Are-You-Ready-to-be-Awakened

[150] http://www.oprah.com/oprahsbookclub/Your-Personal-Workbook-for-A-New-Earth

[151] http://www.oprah.com/oprahsbookclub/A-New-Earth-Exercises-for-Your-Awakening

[152] http://www.closertotruth.com/video-profile/Are-Enlightenment-Transcendence-Altered-States-Charles-T-Tart-/1467

[153] http://www.closertotruth.com/video-profile/Are-Enlightenment-Transcendence-Altered-States-Jaron-Lanier-/1290

Are Enlightenment and Transcendence Altered States (video by Roger Walsh) Part 1 [154]

Are Enlightenment and Transcendence Altered States (video by Roger Walsh) Part 2 [155]

Are Enlightenment and Transcendence Altered States (video by Ananda Guruge) [156]

Are Enlightenment and Transcendence Altered States (video by Mike Merzenich) [157]

Becoming God: The World Is What You Make It [158]

Becoming Galactic Blog: The Four Most Toxic Thought Patterns [159]

---

[154] http://www.closertotruth.com/video-profile/Are-Enlightenment-Transcendence-Altered-States-Part-1-of-2-Roger-Walsh-/1216
[155] http://www.closertotruth.com/video-profile/Are-Enlightenment-Transcendence-Altered-States-Part-2-of-2-Roger-Walsh-/1215
[156] http://www.closertotruth.com/video-profile/Are-Enlightenment-Transcendence-Altered-States-Ananda-Guruge-/1209
[157] http://www.closertotruth.com/video-profile/Are-Enlightenment-Transcendence-Altered-States-Mike-Merzenich-/519
[158] http://www.becominggod.org/home.html
[159] http://www.becoming-galactic.org/fourtoxic.html

Cathars & Catareen: History, Society, Religion and Myth [160]

Consciousness and Substance: The Primal Forms of God [161]

Consciousness, Witnessing and Awareness [162]

Disciple of the Light [163]

Free the Slaves [164]

Gaia Hubs [165]

Global Oneness Project [166]

I AM (the documentary by Tom Shadyac) [167]

---

[160] http://lespiraldelconeixement.com/dostema.cfm?id=19
[161] http://www.colinandrews.net/Consciousness-Article05-JohnWhite.html
[162]

http://www.activemeditation.com/ActiveMeditations/Aspects/Consciousness.html
[163] http://www.disciplelight.com/
[164] http://www.freetheslaves.net/
[165] http://hubs.gaia.com/
[166] http://www.globalonenessproject.org/
[167] http://iamthedoc.com

Invisible Children [168]

Quantum Unlimited [169]

Meditation Station [170]

States of Consciousness [171]

Techniques for Ego-Transcendence [172]

The Art of Now: Six Steps to Living in the Moment [173]

The Christ Mind (author Robert A. Clark) [174]

The Essene Gospels of Peace [175]

---

[168] http://www.invisiblechildren.com/
[169] http://quantumunlimited.org/vem/articles-english-mainmenu-82/
[170] http://www.meditationsociety.com/index.html
[171] http://www.mahalo.com/consciousness/
[172] http://www.ananda.org/meditation/support/articles/ego-transcendance.html
[173] http://www.psychologytoday.com/articles/200810/the-art-now-six-steps-living-in-the-moment
[174] http://www.thechristmind.org/index.htm
[175]
http://www.thenazareneway.com/index_essene_gospels_of_peace.htm

The Forgiveness Web [176]

The Gnostic Society Library: Cathar Texts [177]

The Isha System [178]

The Mystic: Keys to Higher Consciousness [179]

The Stream of Consciousness [180]

The Words of Oneness through Rasha [181]

The Worlds of David Darling [182]

TWM Reference Index (a monumental library) [183]

---

[176] http://www.forgivenessweb.com/
[177] http://www.gnosis.org/library/cathtx.htm
[178]
http://www.whywalkwhenyoucanfly.com/new/contenido.php?seccion
=home
[179] http://www.themystic.org/begin/index.htm
[180] http://quantumunlimited.org/vem/articles-english-mainmenu-
82/1599-the-stream-of-consciousness
[181] http://www.onenesswebsite.com/
[182]
http://www.daviddarling.info/works/ZenPhysics/ZenPhysics_front_2.html
[183] http://twm.co.nz/ind3.html

Vedic Wisdom and Evolution of Consciousness [184]

Veritas Publishing (books by David R. Hawkins) [185]

---

[184] http://www.chakranews.com/vedic-wisdom-and-the-evolutionary-path-of-consciousness/1047

[185] http://www.veritaspub.com/

Michele Doucette is webmistress of Portals of Spirit, a spirituality website whereby one will find links to (1) The Enlightened Scribe, (2) an ezine called Gateway To The Soul, (3) books of spiritual resonance as well as authors of metaphysical importance, (4) categories of interest from Angels to Zen, (5) up-to-date information as shared by a Quantum Healer, (6) affiliate programs and resources of personal significance, (7) healing resource advertisements and (8) spiritual news.

As a Level 2 Reiki Practitioner, she sends long distance Reiki to those who make the request, claiming only to be a facilitator of the Universal energy, meaning that it is up to the individual(s) in question to use these energies in order to heal themselves.

Having also acquired a Crystal Healing Practitioner diploma (Stonebridge College in the UK), she is guardian to many from the mineral kingdom.

She is the author of several spiritual/metaphysical works; namely, *The Ultimate Enlightenment For 2012: All We Need Is Ourselves, Turn Off The TV: Turn On Your Mind, Veracity At Its Best, The Collective: Essays on Reality* (a composition of essays in relation to the Matrix), *Sleepers Awaken: The Time Is Now To Consciously Create Your Own Reality, Healing the Planet and Ourselves: How To Raise Your Vibration* and *You Are Everything: Everything Is You,* all of which have been published through St. Clair Publications.

In addition, she has written a separate volume that deals with crystals, aptly entitled *The Wisdom of Crystals.*

She is also the author of *A Travel in Time to Grand Pré,* a visionary metaphysical novel that historically ties the descendants of Yeshua (Jesus) to modern day Nova Scotia.

As shared by a reviewer, it is *Veracity At Its Best,* a spiritual (metaphysical) tome, that "constructs the context for the spiritual message" imparted in *A Travel in Time to Grand Pré.*

Against the backdrop of 1754 Acadie, it was the blending of French Acadian history with current DNA testing that contributed to the weaving of this alchemical tale of time travel, romance and intrigue.

From Henry I Sinclair to the Merovingians, from the Cathari treasure at Montségur to the Knights Templar, this novel, together with the words of Yeshua as spoken at the height of his ministry, has the potential to inspire others; for it is herein that we learn how individuals can find their way, their truth(s), so as to live their lives to the fullest.

Made in the USA
San Bernardino, CA
14 October 2017